LEAN

Business Analysis
for Agile Teams

**Introducing Lean Principles that Supercharge
Your Requirements Discovery Process
in Agile and Traditional Software Development**

Thomas Hathaway
Angela Hathaway

Ordering Information:

Quantity sales. Special discounts are available on quantity purchases by corporations, associations, and others. For details, contact the publisher at books@BusinessAnalysisExperts.com.

ISBN: 9798616146175

CONTENTS

FROM THE AUTHOR

We would like to acknowledge the thousands of students with whom we have had the honor of working over the years. We can honestly say that every single one of you influenced us in no small way.

As a team, we have trained, consulted, mentored, and coached the latest business analysis techniques to thousands of people in all walks of life around the world. We have worked with organizations from small businesses to Fortune 100.

It is from that experience that we gain the insight and knowledge to author our books and courses. Over the past 30 years, there have been many changes in the world of Business Analysis.

When we started the journey in the late 80's, most organizations had not heard of "Business Analysis". At that time, programmers or system analysts explored the business needs and started programming.

Much has changed since then, and we feel honored to have been part of the group that made this change happen. Over the years, we expanded our Business Analysis Bag of Tricks (BABOT) by learning and adapting business analysis techniques. We have expanded our BABOT with techniques "borrowed" from other disciplines and fields of endeavor where they fit.

As Requirements Solutions Group (now BA-EXPERTS), we experienced the birth of the International Institute of Business Analysis™ (IIBA®) and were among the early "Endorsed Education Providers" (EEP). We reviewed the first and second edition of the BABOK which generated ideas in us how we could use our new-found knowledge to enhance our business analysis courses.

PREFACE

Over the years, Business Analysis has come a long way. Every so often on this journey, we heard the claim "Business Analysis is dead". It never happened. Today, we hear this claim again from the new Lean and Agile world.

We say categorically: "No, it is not dead and never will be!". There will always be a need for someone to define what a digital solution should do from the business perspective. However, WHO fills this role can change at any time and future practitioners could profit from the evolving fields of Artificial Intelligence (AI) and Data Sciences.

Defining Business Needs for Digital Solutions

The single largest challenge facing organizations around the world is how to leverage their Information Technology to gain competitive advantage. This is not about how to program the devices; **it is figuring out what the devices should do.**

Communicating business needs to a technical audience is not a simple activity that organizations need every now and then. It is an ongoing process of evaluating where you are today and deciding where you want to be tomorrow.

Because of that, we always will need some form of business needs analysis. However, Business Analysis must change and adapt like it has every time we found new and more efficient ways of developing software and digital solutions.

The Move to Lean Business Analysis

Nowadays, the Agile and Lean movement drives much of the change in Business Analysis. The Lean movement has touched many different fields. It started in manufacturing and in today's world you find it everywhere (we even found a book titled "Lean Hospitals" at amazon).

The only way for Business Analysis to survive in this new world is to apply Lean principles. In this book, our goal is to get you started on the path to LEAN Business Analysis.

In today's world, you and your organization must be responsive, flexible, and make things happen quickly. You must do more with less – and faster. You no longer have business as usual, so **why do business analysis as usual?**

With the widespread adoption of Agile, software development has gone through some serious remodeling. Agile teams build robust products incrementally and iteratively, needing fast feedback from the business community to define ongoing work.

As a result, the process of defining IT requirements is evolving rapidly. Backlogs replace Requirements Definition Documents. User Stories, Epics and Features replace Requirement Statements. Scenarios and Examples replace Test Cases. The timing of Business Analysis activities is shifting like sand.

What You Will Learn

This book presents **a brief overview** of how you can reduce waste in Business Analysis practices to optimally support the new Lean and Agile software development world. You will learn about topics such as:

- ☑ Agile and Lean thinking applied to Requirements Discovery / Analysis and Acceptance Testing

- ☑ Lean software development methodologies – Kanban, Scrum, Continuous Delivery, ATDD, BDD and how they affect Business Analysis

- ☑ Potential wastes in Business Analysis and Lean principles to combat them

- ☑ Lean requirement constructs such as Features, User Stories, Epics, Scenarios, etc.

- ☑ Product Backlogs, Kanban Boards, and other requirements repositories

- ☑ The purpose of a Product Roadmap and a prioritized Product Backlog

- ☑ The concept of a Minimum Viable Product (MVP)

☑ A bird's eye view of Lean Business Analysis techniques, such as Lean communications techniques, Cynefin Framework, Pain-point Analysis, Story Splitting, Functional Drilldown, Lean Use Cases, and more

☑ Acceptance or Business-Facing Testing (ATDD)

HOW DO LEAN PRINCIPLES AFFECT THE BUSINESS ANALYSIS PROCESS?

Business Needs Discovery and Analysis in Agile Software Development

The concept of doing things "Lean" has become exceedingly popular in recent years. Lean thinking is a phenomenally interesting and effective philosophy for getting things done faster while delivering added value or benefits.

In today's world, you will find Lean approaches in most disciplines. The concept originated in manufacturing. It is also applied in many other areas such as start-ups, sales, and – yes – software development. Mary and Tom Poppendieck coined the term "Lean software development" in 2003.

However, two years earlier, the manifesto for Agile Development was published in 2001. It is celebrated by many as the entry into Lean Software Development. In today's world the terms Lean and Agile are often used interchangeably, albeit erroneously.

Lean and Agile software development approaches have been adopted across the board as a way of developing and delivering valuable working software to the business.

> However, these approaches are **NOT** a means for identifying business needs or stakeholder requirements.

Applying Lean Thinking
to Business Analysis

In the early years of Lean and Agile software development, using requirements definition techniques that were developed to support a traditional (most often Waterfall) methodology resulted in lots of waste.

WASTE OF RESOURCES
WASTE OF DEVELOPMENT TIME
WASTE OF EFFORT

Studies have shown that many projects delivered only 15 to 25 percent of requirements that had been defined in the Business Requirements Document. That implies that 75 to 80% of the work done in capturing, defining, documenting, prioritizing, discussing, and communicating the remaining requirements was a total waste.

Over time, many companies realized that Lean thinking must not only be applied to the software development process but also to detailed requirements discovery, analysis, and acceptance testing.

For that reason, the process of defining software requirements from a business perspective is evolving rapidly:

- ☑ **Backlogs** replace Business Requirements Documents (BRD's)
- ☑ **User Stories**, **Epics** and **Features** replace requirement statements
- ☑ **Scenarios** and **Examples** replace test cases
- ☑ The **timing** of Business Analysis activities is shifting like sand
- ☑ **Who** does Business Analysis tasks is also changing dramatically

Who Does Business Analysis in Your Organization?

Many IT initiatives no longer use a Business Analyst but require that Product Owners, Subject Matter Experts, and many other roles or job titles have Business Analysis skills. Companies realize that the skills needed to identify and define the best digital solutions are invaluable for every role in the organization.

Since there are several Lean concepts in use by today's software developers, you, as the one wearing the BA hat, need to understand enough about the various Lean and Agile development approaches to decide which Business Analysis techniques and activities you need to use in each approach.

A Bird's Eye View of Four LEAN Software Development Philosophies

You can find never-ending definitions online about Lean software development approaches. For the purpose of this book (and even more important, for Business Analysts), we will explore four basic philosophies and the primary methodology of each. The four philosophies that domineer the world of IT today are:

⇨ **LEAN**

⇨ **AGILE**

⇨ **CONTINUOUS DELIVERY**

⇨ **CONTINUOUS INTEGRATION**

Lean and Kanban

Organizations can use a Lean approach for any business process or function - whether it is software development, IT/Ops, Staffing, Recruitment, Marketing and Sales, Procurement, etc. Every time, however, the focus is on:

---

eliminating waste

delivering value to the end-user or customer

The Kanban Method is a widely used Lean approach to gradually improve any business function. Kanban is not a software development methodology, but the principles of Kanban are often applied to **existing** software development processes.

Kanban is the Japanese word for billboard or sign. A Kanban Board, the pivotal point of this approach, is a way of making work visible so that you can more easily identify bottlenecks and recognize where waste can be eliminated.

Agile and Scrum

Many folks use the terms Lean and Agile interchangeably. However, the **Agile** philosophy focuses exclusively on software development. The most widely used Agile methodology is Scrum.

At the heart of Scrum is the Agile Team with their "Agile Ceremonies" (i.e. Standups, Release Planning, Sprint Planning, Retrospectives, etc.). All Agile Teams are on a fixed iteration schedule with formal planning.

An Agile Team can use other Lean methodologies such as Kanban (and many do), however, Agile is a concept from the software development world and focuses primarily on delivering working software to the customer as quickly as possible.

Many Agile software teams use Kanban to prioritize and deliver work items, improve collaboration, and reduce delays as well as unnecessary or unimportant work. Later, we will have a lot more about what Scrum is and how it works.

Continuous Delivery and DevOps

A third philosophy that affects how we develop and deliver information technology is Continuous Delivery. This is an approach to build software in a manner that it can be released into production at any time.

Here is an analogy. Imagine you are living in a house and you want new paint on your walls. Would you move out of your house, burn the thing down, build a new house, and paint your walls in a new color?

That is how we used to deliver software. Sounds pretty stupid nowadays, doesn't it? Wouldn't it be much easier to continue living in the house and simply change and improve it? That is the whole idea behind Continuous Delivery.

It is based on the theory that the ongoing development of software is an integral component of the operations of any organization. These two critical business processes cannot and should not be separated.

The primary methodology associated with Continuous Delivery is DevOps which is about combining the two areas - Software Development and Software Operations/Maintenance. This allows users to utilize the software without any problems while it is being maintained / updated. That was not possible in traditional software development approaches.

Continuous Integration and ATDD/BDD

Continuous Integration puts emphasis on automating the testing process. It is almost a pre-requisite for successful implementation of Continuous Delivery. Continuous Integration assures that the new application or the latest changes that you have made are working for the entire organization.

The primary methodology that is associated with Continuous Integration is Automated Test-Driven Development (ATDD) or Behavior-Driven Development (BDD). In companies using modern software development approaches, Acceptance Tests ARE the ultimate requirements that developers implement. We will spend much more time on these two approaches later in this book.

Using techniques such as Continuous Delivery and Continuous Integration, organizations can implement thousands of changes in a very short time. For example, Amazon reportedly releases 23,000 changes to their software daily in 2019. That is a true implementation of Continuous Delivery and Continuous Integration.

In Summary

This was a brief overview of the most common modern software development philosophies.

Philosophy	Primary Focus	Primary Methodology
Lean	*Eliminate Waste*	Kanban
Agile	*Software Production*	Scrum
Continuous Delivery	*Continuity*	DevOps
Continuous Integration	*Software Quality*	ATDD/BDD

They all are based on Lean Thinking and our traditional approach to Business Analysis no longer fits with these methods. It is time we apply Lean Thinking to Business Analysis.

To that end, the question becomes:

Where does waste hide in traditional Business Analysis?

Potential Wastes in Business Analysis and Requirements Discovery

The web is full of stories that describe wasted effort in creating a Business Requirements Document which is usually the outcome of traditional Business Analysis activities.

Based on feedback from thousands of students and our consulting engagements, we identified the following items that represent waste in the traditional Business Analysis process.

Requirements Completed, Not Implemented

A big waste in the BA world is defining requirements that never make it into production. Just imagine the effort that it takes you to gather a user requirement, analyze the requirement, document it, communicate it to the development team, and then figure out how to test whether it is implemented correctly.

Now imagine that after all that work, that requirement never gets implemented. You just wasted a ton of effort!

Defining Features Customers Do Not Use

In 2002, The Standish Group discovered that, on average, only 20 percent of the features that an application offered were always or, at least often, used. Another 16 percent were used sometimes but the vast majority of the of the features (64%) were rarely or never used.

This statistic has not changed much over the years. In 2014, the Standish Group reported that 50% of features were hardly ever used.

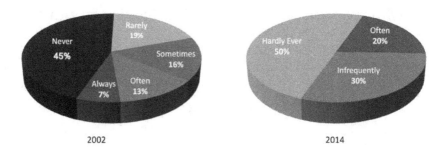

2002   2014

Not only is there a lot of waste for the developers, all Business Analysis effort that went into the software to deliver those features was wasted effort as well.

Working Without a Common Understanding.

The most important job of a Business Analyst (BA) is to communicate business needs to the technical teams. If the BA and the business community do not share a mutual understanding, the resulting business requirements will be ambiguous, error prone, conflicting, and maybe even plain wrong. Obviously, this will result in a huge amount of wasted time and effort.

Doing Work That Does Not Add Value

If a feature or business requirement does not add value from a user or customer perspective, analyzing and defining the feature is a waste of time and effort.

For example, a creative BA might decide that adding a feature to a mobile app that would allow the user to place a call directly by clicking on a phone number is a neat feature to have.

But does this feature really bring value to your end-user? It would be a waste of effort to define the feature if your end-user says no.

Moving from One Task to the Next Without Focus

This sounds like a Business Analyst with ADD but it is just part of being a BA. There always are interruptions and you switch tasks because of changing priorities. Unfortunately, every time you switch activities there is a thing called "ramp time".

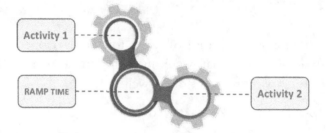

Ramp time is the time it takes you to make sure that you can pick up the old task where you left off and prepare to work on the new task . If you do this without focus, moving from one task to another causes a lot of waste.

Waiting for an Answer or Availability

We all know this one. Sometimes, we just cannot continue our work without a decision, an answer, or a resource to become available. Sitting around twiddling our thumbs waiting for things to happen is certainly a huge waste of time.

Work That Needs to Be Redone

This one is obvious. Any time a BA, Product Owner, or SME defines a business need incorrectly or the developers interpret the requirement incorrectly or software fails to pass appropriate tests, most, if not all work, must be redone. Having to redo anything is a primary waste of time, effort, and other resources.

Keeping Knowledge to Yourself

Another way of looking at waste is hiding knowledge. For example, if SMEs are afraid of losing their job, they might not share all their knowledge. That leads to missing or incorrect business requirements. Another example is experts who want to do everything themselves and do not share their knowledge or expertise.

Both situations lead to waste. In one you will miss pertinent information leading to errors and work that needs to be redone. In the other, you will experience a bottleneck.

Unused Human Creativity

The final kind of waste is unused human creativity. This happens when an organization does not take full advantage of skills that their employees have.

These types of waste are the major culprits that cause us to spend a lot of time and money when defining business requirements for a digital solution.

Requirements Completed, Not Implemented	Defining Features Customers Do Not Use	Working Without a Common Understanding
Doing Things That Do Not Add Value	Moving From One Task To Next Without Focus	Waiting For an Answer or Availability
Work That Needs To Be Redone	Keeping Knowledge To Yourself	Unused Human Creativity

Now that we have pinpointed several distinct types of waste in Business Analysis, how can we eliminate or at least alleviate that waste and get closer to "Lean Business Analysis"?

6 Lean Principles to Combat Waste in Business Analysis

Lean Principles Applied to Business Analysis

There are 6 basic Lean principles that you can use for any process or workflow to make them "leaner", meaning more efficient while adding value. In this chapter, we will apply these 6 Lean principles to the process of conducting Business Analysis.

1. Deliver Appropriate Details Just-in-Time (JIT)

Just-in-Time (JIT) is one of the fundamental principles of Lean. JIT means that you never do anything until you absolutely need to.

For example, a company that sells office furniture only manufactures the furniture (or orders it from another manufacturer) when a customer makes a purchase.

In the world of Business Analysis, it means that we do not deliver a detailed User Story with Acceptance Criteria and Tests until the developers are ready to program that story. Try not do things too early in the project or product lifecycle. **Do them Just-in-Time!**

2. Deliver Only What Is Needed and Not More

The first part of this principle is straight forward. If we try to give people a lot of features, we end up delivering features that they do not need which is a form of waste.

Including the business value in your requirements is a big step in the right direction. This allows everyone to evaluate the need for this feature.

There is a second part to this principle. For example, if you are filling a product backlog, your User Story or requirement should have just enough detail so that everyone understands what it is and can discuss the Story or business need.

However, when you are providing requirements for the next Sprint or Iteration, your User Story or requirement needs a lot more detail (which can be in writing or in discussions with the developers).

Let's take this principle even a step further. Imagine that in our example from principle 1, your developer is ready for your User Story and wants to program it. If s/he is an experienced programmer with lots of domain knowledge, Lean Business Analysis means that you would adapt the level of detail to that person's domain knowledge. You always prepare your User Stories only as detailed as your technical team needs to deliver the feature.

3. Work with the Right People at the Right Time

Working with the right people at the right time is a critical part of Lean Business Analysis. If you get the wrong people involved, you will have wrong decisions and delays which cause rework

Since identifying the right Stakeholders for your project or initiative plays a vital role in eliminating waste, make sure that your Business Analysts have excellent stakeholder analysis techniques in their Business Analysis bag of techniques and tricks.

4. Build Quality in From the Outset

Ensuring that the product has the necessary quality is another fundamental principle of Lean. It is challenging or impossible to build quality into a product once it is built. If you need to sacrifice quality to eliminate waste, it is not Lean. Lean production means eliminating waste **while** delivering quality products to avoid rework and/or customer complaints.

5. Avoid Unnecessary Non-Value Adding Activities

In Lean Business Analysis, as in most Lean approaches, activities in an organization are grouped into value-added (VA) activities and non-value-added (NVA) activities. Six Sigma says it best:

For something to add value, three things must happen:

1. The activity or the step must change the form or function of the product or service under development
2. The customer must be willing to pay for the change
3. The step must be performed correctly the first time

Anything that does not accomplish this is a waste – or non-value added. This can involve everything from workers having to take too many steps on the manufacturing floor to office workers duplicating paperwork.

If an activity does not have all three components, chances are it is a **non-value-adding activity** and should be avoided or reduced.

Sometimes whether an activity is value-added or non-value-added is hard to answer. Let your judgement be your guide. But do not waste your time doing things that do not directly add value to someone who uses the product.

6. Practice Active Collaboration and Knowledge Sharing

There is a wealth of knowledge within each organization. All too often, this knowledge is either simply not shared or you have a knowledge hoarding problem.

Working together is often a key success criterion for Lean initiatives. Knowledge sharing and cross-functional collaboration brings many benefits to an organization.

The Lean philosophy assumes that the work you are doing is also a learning process for everyone involved.

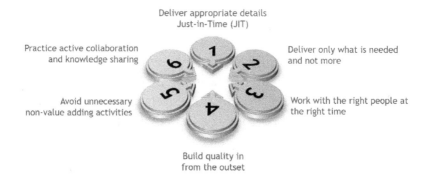

Deliver appropriate details
Just-in-Time (JIT)

Practice active collaboration
and knowledge sharing

Deliver only what is needed
and not more

Avoid unnecessary
non-value adding activities

Work with the right people at
the right time

Build quality in
from the outset

How Lean Principles Cut Down on Wasteful Business Analysis Work

Bringing it all together, we can see which of the six Lean principles primarily cut each type of waste in business analysis.

WASTE 1:

⊠ Requirements Completed, Not Implemented

LEAN PRINCIPLE:

☑ Deliver appropriate details Just-in-Time (JIT)
☑ Deliver only what is needed and not more

Delivering details just in time and only describing the level of detail needed for the next Business Analysis activity reduces waste caused by Business Analysts supplying too much detail too early. User Stories or other requirements that someone defines in detail too early are a significant waste if those same requirements are eliminated later.

WASTE 2:

⊠ Defining Features Customers Do Not Use

LEAN PRINCIPLE:

- ☑ Deliver only what is needed and not more
- ☑ Work with the right people at the right time

We can cut down on a lot of waste in business analysis if we deliver **only** what our stakeholders "really" need. Techniques such as defining a Minimum Viable Product help with this task. In addition, selecting our stakeholders carefully using stakeholder analysis techniques also cuts down on waste.

WASTE 3:

- ☒ Working Without a Common Understanding

LEAN PRINCIPLE:

- ☑ Work with the right people at the right time
- ☑ Practice active collaboration and knowledge sharing more

If you practice active collaboration and knowledge sharing, your chances that everybody understands what the digital solution will deliver increase exponentially (assuming you are working with the right people at the right time).

WASTE 4:

- ☒ Doing Things That Do Not Add Value

LEAN PRINCIPLE:

- ☑ Deliver only what is needed and not more
- ☑ Avoid unnecessary non-value adding activities

If you focus on your customers' strongest desires and needs, you will save a lot of time and money. Who knows, it might just get you that promotion you deserve.

Combine this with working mostly on value-added tasks *(customers are willing to pay for the outcome of what you do)* while reducing non-value-added tasks *(customers will not pay for the outcome)* and you are surely on the road to low garbage, sorry, I mean low waste production. Good prioritization techniques and lean requirements analysis techniques go a long way to achieve this goal.

WASTE 5:

⊠ Moving from One Task to Next Without Focus

LEAN PRINCIPLE:

☑ Build quality in from the outset
☑ Avoid unnecessary non-value adding activities

If you are moving from task to task without focus, you are wasting a ton of ramp time and increasing the probability of errors. That requires rework and adds to the waste. Without focus, it is nearly impossible to deliver a product with the required level of quality.

WASTE 6:

⊠ Waiting for an Answer or Availability

LEAN PRINCIPLE:

☑ Work with the right people at the right time
☑ Avoid unnecessary non-value adding activities

Waiting for an answer or availability sure sounds like a non-value-added activity. Do not wait long for either, use lean business analysis techniques and involve the right people at the right time to give you the answers you need. This will eliminate or at least drastically reduce the wait time.

WASTE 7:

⊠ Work That Needs to Be Redone

LEAN PRINCIPLE:

☑ Deliver appropriate details Just-in-Time (JIT)
☑ Build quality in from the outset

By doing things just-in-time (read "last responsible moment"), and building quality in from the get-go, you minimize the re-work that must be done.

WASTE 8:

⊠ Keeping Knowledge to Yourself

LEAN PRINCIPLE:

☑ Work with the right people at the right time
☑ Practice active collaboration and knowledge sharing more

Keeping knowledge to yourself is a noticeably big waste for you and your company. It might seem beneficial at first, but practicing active collaboration and knowledge sharing with the right people at the right time will have major advantages for you in a Lean environment.

WASTE 9:

⊠ Unused Human Creativity

LEAN PRINCIPLE:

☑ Practice active collaboration and knowledge sharing

And here again, practicing active collaboration allows all of us to use our creativity to take advantage of what other people know. However, don't forget, knowledge sharing is a two-way street.

Lean Success Criteria
Defer decision until the last moment
Just-in-Time (JIT) deliverables
Deliver ONLY essentials
Right people, right time
Build in quality
Avoid non-essential work
Active collaboration

The Shift of Focus
from Project to Product Thinking

Project vs. Product Thinking

One of the biggest changes (and for many the most difficult change) in a Lean and Agile environment is shifting the focus from project thinking to product thinking.

Mik Kersten of Tasktop makes an exceptionally good point in his book "Project to Product" when he writes that,

> "in today's world, it is important to realize that all companies are software companies. As such, IT is no longer a project-based enabler but a part of the product team".

This is a fundamental shift in philosophy because projects are a collection of activities and tasks that we do to develop products (or services which are a type of product). Products are outcomes that a customer buys and uses.

To put it another way, the biggest difference between project and product thinking is that projects are limited by resources whereas products are limited by capabilities.

Project management focuses on delivery.

Product development focuses on the outcome.

This is a significant shift from project thinking to product thinking. Rather than focusing on timelines and dates, we focus on how to make the product the best it can be.

Adopting a Product Mindset

If we adopt a product mindset, we can learn and adapt as we go which increases our chances for highly satisfied customers over time.

In the past, many Agile teams were convinced that there is no need for a Business Analyst in a product-driven approach. True, you do not need someone with the "job title" Business Analyst on your development team.

However, someone on your Agile team better have a solid set of business analysis techniques handy. Otherwise, your feature discovery process and, consequently, your Product Backlog might become a roadblock in your move towards business agility.

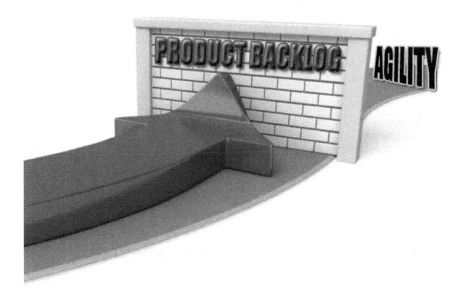

Fortunately, there is a growing acceptance of business analysis tasks and techniques on Lean and Agile teams as well as a recognition that doing them supplies value and better outcomes.

Product Thinking Supports Business Agility

The goal of product thinking is to shift the focus of your team from thinking about what tasks they need to finish to how to get the product to be the best it can be in the shortest time possible.

Obviously, the better the input into your development team (meaning the Features, User Stories, and other requirements), the more successful your move from project to product will be.

The tremendous success rates of Agile initiatives that focus on product and not project is proof that product thinking is the best way - the only way - to achieve business agility and shorten time to market.

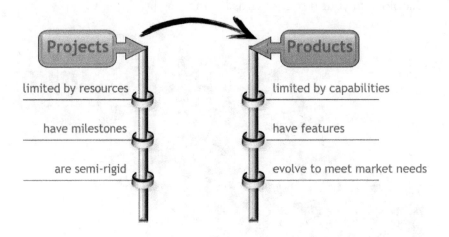

Projects	Products
limited by resources	limited by capabilities
have milestones	have features
are semi-rigid	evolve to meet market needs

Shifting Focus from Milestones to Features

Another difference that has a major impact on the requirements discovery process is that projects have milestones whereas products have features. This change has major repercussion for the Business Analyst. We must adapt business analysis techniques to this change in thinking.

Lean Business Analysis Embraces Change

The last difference we want to mention is that projects are semi-rigid meaning they have a defined scope, timeframe, and budget which are difficult to change whereas products evolve to meet market needs.

You might start developing a product thinking that it will only be of interest for a brief time. Suddenly you realize that the demand is so great, and the feedback you receive gives you more and more ideas how to evolve this product. Having the focus on product instead of project allows it to evolve and integrate features that people want and need as usage of it evolves.

Having the focus on traditional project objectives (as opposed to product objectives) quite often is detrimental to the product quality. And remember one of the Lean principles is build quality in from the get-go. Trying to follow a rigid project schedule can counteract that.

LEAN REQUIREMENTS ARE THE ULTIMATE GOAL OF LEAN BUSINESS ANALYSIS

The Need for LEAN Requirements

Traditional Requirements Are Rigid and Complete from the Start

Traditionally, Business Analysts (or whoever defined business requirements) elicited or gathered, analyzed, documented, and managed all user and system requirements **at the beginning** of a project. Methodologies such as Waterfall or structured methods started each project with an analysis phase.

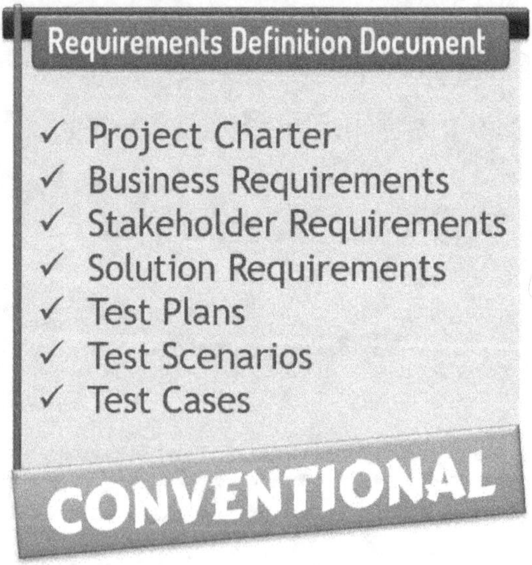

Requirements Definition Document

- ✓ Project Charter
- ✓ Business Requirements
- ✓ Stakeholder Requirements
- ✓ Solution Requirements
- ✓ Test Plans
- ✓ Test Scenarios
- ✓ Test Cases

CONVENTIONAL

It often took months to define a complete set of detailed software specifications for the entire application in a Business Requirements Document (BRD).

These requirements were more or less set in stone once the analysis phase was completed until the solution was implemented. They could only be modified through obligatory and highly complex change management processes.

Lean Requirements Are Flexible and Just-In-Time

Lean requirements, on the other hand, must be easily changeable at ANY point in time. In addition, Lean requirements must ALWAYS be limited to the level of detail necessary to support ONLY the next imminent decision(s).

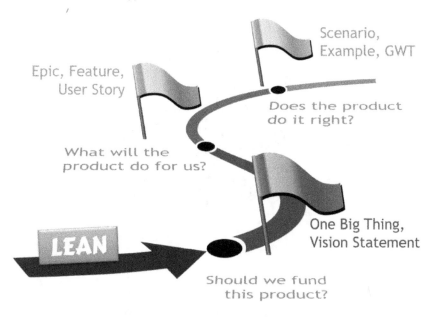

This is a novel concept! Think about it! To grasp the product vision and make good business decisions along the way, we do not need software specifications or solution-level requirements.

Once a developer starts programming, s/he might need incredibly detailed software specifications. However, even that depends on the experience of the programmer. During the Agile development process, Lean requirements must facilitate discussions amongst the business and developer communities.

Lean Requirements Must Be Testable

Finally, a Lean requirement must be testable, meaning the business community can validate each feature or function as soon as they are programmed (more on that later).

As many Agile teams found out, traditional "requirements" did not work well (or did not work at all) in an Agile software development environment.

Conventional Requirements Levels

To understand the brave new world of Lean/Agile Business Analysis and Lean requirements in context, here is a brief refresher on conventional IT requirements.

According to the International Institute for Business Analysis™ (IIBA®), there are three fundamental levels at which we define requirements for IT projects:

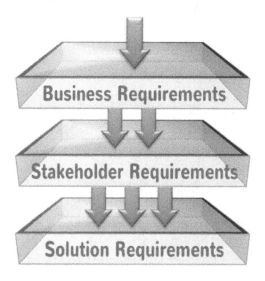

Business Requirements

A Business Requirement, according to the IIBA®, is a high-level business need stating goals and objectives that will benefit the whole organization or a large group thereof. For example,

"Waste-the-Waste will increase our customer base by 20 percent by the end of the fiscal year."

Stakeholder Requirements

A Stakeholder Requirement, the next level of detail, talks about the needs and wants of individuals or a group of people who share common responsibilities. For example,

---

"As a website visitor, I can order any product in Waste-the-Waist's catalog directly from the site to reduce ordering time."

Solution Requirements

However, to develop an application, developers and technical teams often need detailed software specifications. The IIBA defines this level as Solution Requirements. Solution-level requirements are functional and non-functional details of HOW Business and Stakeholder Requirements will be implemented.

A good example of a functional requirement is,

"Calculate product price including fees and taxes."

A non-functional type of a requirement would be something like,

---

"Average response time will be less than 3 seconds."

Lean Requirements Still Need All 3 Levels but . . .

Business, Stakeholder, and Solution Requirements are critical for delivering high quality digital solutions. They are still critical in a Lean and Agile environment but, as mentioned earlier, the timing of the levels of details is shifted to the last responsible moment.

In addition, several new ways of writing and communicating the three levels have evolved to support agile development.

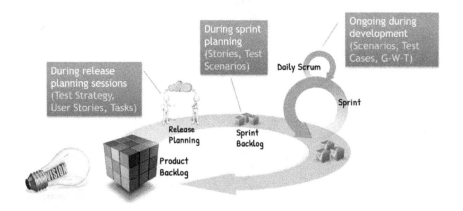

Requirements Constructs in an Agile/Lean Environment

Moving into a Lean and Agile environment, the nature of the requirements that we are defining changes. To support a lean development team in its activities, we need new requirements constructs such as,

→ Features
→ Epics
→ User Stories
→ Lean Use Cases
→ Business Rules
→ Constraints
→ Scenarios (GWT)
→ Examples

You might recognize some of them from the conventional requirements world.

Features, Epics, and User Stories

The first three in this list – Features, Epics, and User Stories – are the most common constructs or types of requirements in Agile development. They are also the ones that create the most confusion.

If you google "what is a Feature", "what is an Epic", or "what is a User Story", you get so many different explanations and points of view that your head will spin.

The reason is there are many different (and right) ways to define the same word depending on your framework. Fortunately, it is not important what you call them. All three of them (in any software development framework) are levels of hierarchy.

Unfortunately, in some companies you might have to spend your time on a semantic argument about the difference between Features, Epics, and User Stories. With that in mind, here is **our** answer to the question "what are …?".

The Most Common Hierarchy

Let's start at the bottom of the hierarchy. The requirement construct with the most detail is the **USER STORY**. A User Story describes the WHO, WHAT, and WHY of a desired functionality.

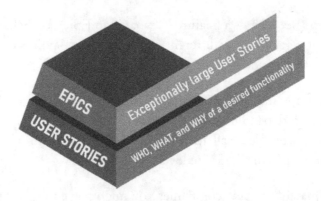

At the next higher level, we find **EPICS** which are exceptionally large User Stories that the development team considers too complex to fit in one release (in Agile, a release is an event in which production-ready code is migrated from the test into the production environment - more on that later).

FEATURES can be the most confusing. In some organizations, one Feature encompasses multiple User Stories. In other organizations, the Feature is subordinate to the User Story. And there are organizations that ignore the User Story and use Feature drill-down, meaning a high-level feature encompasses multiple lower-level Features.

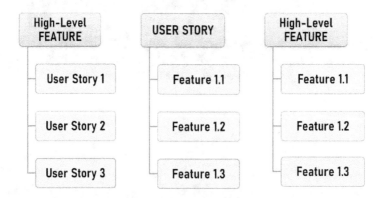

Either way, a Feature is a piece of functionality that delivers business value. Stated another way, a Product Feature in a Lean and Agile environment is any behavior, fact, or dimension of the product that is visible — meaning end-users notice it.

It Doesn't Matter What You Call It

For example, an "Online Shopping Cart" is a Feature. It gives value to the end-user, but it is too complex to be a User Story or low-level Feature. You would have to create a set of User Stories to satisfy this Feature.

This is where the confusion starts. In some companies "Online Shopping Cart" is a Feature in others it is an Epic. Does it really matter what you call it?

The important part about the "Online Shopping Cart" is that you need only the label to add this functionality to your product. The WHO, WHAT, and WHY are self-evident. Writing a User Story would be a waste of time when you are just planning the product development.

The closer you get to implementing this functionality, the more detail (WHO, WHAT, WHY) you need for estimating, coding, and testing purposes.

Lean Business Use Cases

A Use Case is not a new concept, but many analysts still use it in the Lean and Agile world. It depicts how people interact with technology or how two different technologies interact with each other.

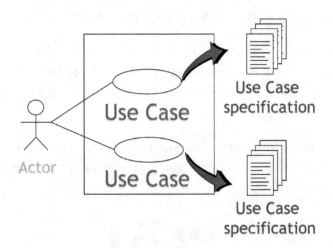

Many Agile purists have decided that Use Cases provide no value for Agile teams. We disagree strongly! True, full-blown Detailed Use Cases might no longer have the value they once had. However, Business Use Cases, Summary Use Cases, and especially Use Case Slices are more important than ever.

(Author's note: we have applied system-level Use Case techniques very successfully in release planning sessions when we were facing a complex set of user interactions).

Business Use Cases are a great tool for giving you context and defining a complete set of needed Features and User Stories. Use Cases also shine when it comes to finding Scenarios for Acceptance Testing.

We have a full course on Lean Use Case development and many of our students love the ideas in it and have successfully implemented them.

User Stories alone often do not give you the context needed for major decision making. Use Cases on the other hand (at the right level of detail) can easily provide an executive view allowing the client leadership to evaluate whether you are heading in the right direction.

However, like with all tools in a Lean and Agile world, Use Cases do not fit all the time. You must decide when it is better to define business needs in Use Case format and when to stick with the simpler User Story format. Obviously, developing a full-blown Detailed Use Case and then creating Features and User Stories is not lean.

Adapt Your Business Needs Definition Every Time

If you decide that Use Cases are the way to go, do not just blindly follow the UML syntax and structure. Decide what level of Use Case is needed and what structure the Use Case requires to serve YOU or your teams' purpose. It is extremely important to realize that Use Cases must follow the LEAN principles too.

At BA-EXPERTS, we have never defined business needs the same way twice because every initiative required a unique approach especially in the Lean and Agile world. Lean Business Analysis means that you are flexible and adapt your analysis techniques to what you need in the moment. For example,

- ☑ For a simple or well-defined user interaction, informal User Stories are probably the best approach.

- ☑ If you are struggling with breaking a complex user interaction down into User Stories, a Use Case Slice might be the easiest and fastest technique to break an Epic down.

Business Rules

Every company has Business Rules. They are the written and unwritten guidelines that dictate how a company conducts its business. Business Rules define how to do business across the entire organization.

Business Rules are pre-established decisions and as such, they fit extremely well into Lean Requirements Constructs. They save everyone from wasting time defining the same requirements or rules repeatedly for every product.

Business Rule Example

For example, many Features and User Stories across multiple products need to communicate with customers via email. If your company accepts valid and invalid email addresses at sign-up, you do not need a Business Rule.

However, if your company has rules as to what makes an email address valid, defining a Feature or User Story every time your product needs a valid email from your customer would be a huge waste of effort.

In this example, you could have two Business Rules:

1. **A customer must have a valid email address**

2. **An email address is valid if it is not returned as 'undeliverable' within 3 hours.**

Just as a side note, not every Business Rule is a simple sentence. For example, complex Business Rules are often represented as a Decision Table (or Decision Tree).

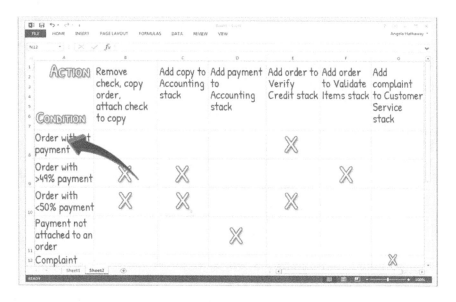

	Remove check, copy order, attach check to copy	Add copy to Accounting stack	Add payment to Accounting stack	Add order to Verify Credit stack	Add order to Validate Items stack	Add complaint to Customer Service stack
ACTION / **CONDITION**						
Order without payment				X		
Order with >49% payment	X	X			X	
Order with <50% payment	X	X		X		
Payment not attached to an order			X			
Complaint						X

This representation of a Business Rule fits very well into Lean and Agile approaches. It is also ideal for discovering Acceptance Tests in Scenario format if you adopt ATDD or BDD.

In the world of Big Data, Business Rules will become even more important since more data often leads to more Business Rules.

Constraints

Constraints are externally mandated restrictions or limits that represent real-world boundaries around a digital solution.

Some examples of Constraints are performance criteria, laws, architectural constraints, the environment, technology that is in use, and things like that. Constraints are also a subcategory of Non-functional Requirement (NFR). They ensure the usability and effectiveness of one or more products.

Many organizations document Constraints as part of the Product Backlog, others maintain a Constraint Backlog. If the Constraint only applies to one User Story, some organizations document the Constraint as Acceptance Criteria of a User Story, others give it its own User Story as in:

**"As a Sales Rep, I want to be able to use
my accumulated contact information
on all versions of Sales Force starting with . . ."**

Scenarios and Scenario Outlines

In Lean and Agile approaches, Acceptance Testing starts as early as possible in the development process. Modern Acceptance Test-Driven Development (ATDD) and Behavior Driven Development (BDD) simplify the testing process.

ATDD and BDD are getting increasingly popular in Lean and Agile environments because automated testing is a pre-requisite for Continuous Delivery and Continuous Integration.

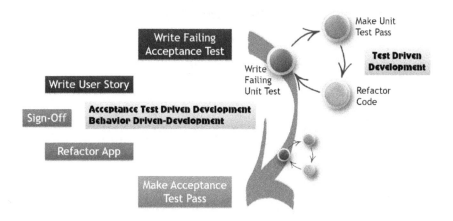

Whether your developers prefer User Stories, Features, or plain textual requirement statements, in a Lean environment, each must have Acceptance Criteria. Acceptance Criteria determine when a User Story or user requirement works as planned from the end-user perspective.

Acceptance Criteria can be written in different formats. One format that has gained wide acceptance is GWT Scenarios (written in Gherkin Given/When/Then syntax).

Scenarios

A Scenario is a concrete example that depicts a specific situation out of real life to prove whether the application does what it should do. Here is an example:

> Scenario: **Fred requests recommended training topics**
>
> GIVEN **Fred is logged in to website**
> And **Fred has completed BASE**
> And **Fred has unfinished training topics**
> WHEN **Fred requests training plan**
> THEN **Fred's customized training plan is viewable**

Since a Scenario can only have a single set of data values, one Acceptance Criteria can result in many Scenarios.

Scenario Outlines

Scenario Outlines are another opportunity to eliminate waste. A Scenario Outline uses variables which are filled from Example tables to minimize unnecessary redundancy. Each row in an Example Table is a specific Scenario. Stackoverflow.com has a funny and simple example of a Scenario Outline:

```
Scenario Outline: Use Blender with <thing>
  Given I put "<thing>" in a blender
  When I switch the blender on
  Then it should transform into "<other thing>"

Examples: Amphibians
        | thing         | other thing |
        | Red Tree Frog | mush        |
        | apples        | apple juice |

Examples: Consumer Electronics
        | thing         | other thing |
        | iPhone        | toxic waste |
        | Galaxy Nexus  | toxic waste |
```

Outcomes of Conventional vs. **LEAN** Business Analysis

Business Analysis or the process of how we define user requirements in a Lean environment has changed. In the old world, we delivered a Business Requirements Document at the beginning of the project. In the new world, we must judge whether requirement details add value or are potential waste.

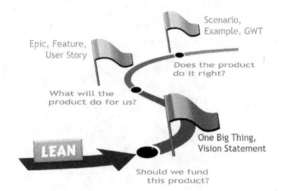 

Although we are still delivering Business, Stakeholder, and Solution Requirements, in Lean and Agile Business Analysis, we create **Lean Requirements Constructs** throughout the development timeline at the point in time when they are needed.

When someone has a new idea for a product or service, the primary decisions we want to make are:

- ◈ Should we fund this product?
- ◈ Is this product a promising idea?

In the old world we would have had a Project Charter and Business Requirements. In the Lean world, we have a Vision Statement, or what many people call affectionately "the next big thing".

Some organizations still call this the Project Charter; but again, the name is of no importance as long as everyone gets a good idea of the goals and objectives that the new product supports.

After someone made the decision to fund the product, we started thinking about what the product could do for the end user or customer. This is where Lean and conventional Business Analysis separate.

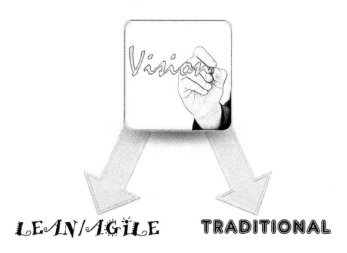

LEAN/AGILE   TRADITIONAL

Traditional Business Analysis

In the old world we would have been defining Stakeholder and Solution Requirements (functional and non-functional software specifications), creating Test Plans, Test Scenarios, and Test Cases, and documenting all of them in a Business Requirements Document (BRD). We did all of this **before** the design or coding of the solution even had started.

The BRD had enough detail to be a guide to the business and technical communities until the whole application was implemented. Defining this level of detail at the beginning of the project (projects often took years) caused a lot of waste because most business needs change over time.

Lean Business Analysis

In the brave new world, we run facilitated workshops using the Vision Statement to discover high-level Features, Epics, and User Stories which we document in a Product Backlog (or some other requirements collection place like a Kanban Board).

The Product Owner, or whoever maintains the Product Backlog, uses business analysis techniques to organize and prioritize Features and/or User Stories. This person also creates a roadmap to have a clear picture.

Changing business needs are always welcome in the Backlog. That fulfills another Lean principle.

When developers are ready to code the next piece of functionality for the product, the Agile team (including the Business Analyst) flesh out the Features, Epics, and User Stories. How far they drill down depends on the organization and the domain knowledge as well as the programming skill-level of the developers.

At the same time, the Business Analyst or the QA team develops Scenarios (and Scenario Outlines if needed) resulting in immediate feedback that the selected product Features or Stories work as planned.

Product Backlogs, Kanban Boards, and Other Requirements Repositories

The traditional Business Requirements Document (BRD) was typically an exceptionally large document that very few people ever read. Quite often it was difficult to find things in it. The shift from project thinking to product thinking did not end the need for documentation. However, a BRD was no longer the right vehicle. It was too bloated causing too much waste.

The biggest and most important change in Lean and Agile is a shift in thinking. We must no longer define requirements to the level of detail developers need without considering WHEN and even IF someone needs this detailed information.

For Lean Business Analysis to succeed, you must take the organizational culture, the skill-level of the technical team, as well as timing (WHEN a certain requirements construct is needed) into account when defining user requirements.

Lean Requirements Repositories (Backlogs) became critically important to achieve these goals.

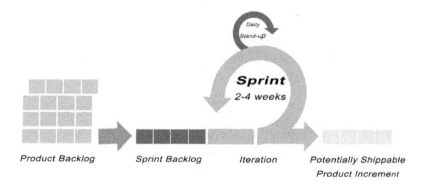

Product Backlog   Sprint Backlog   Iteration   Potentially Shippable Product Increment

Product Requirements Documents (PRD)

PRD's like BRD's are considered by many as an artifact used in traditional software development environments (Waterfall, etc.). There are, however, quite a few organizations that still use traditional PRDs.

There is nothing wrong with this. If PRD's work for you and do not cause any significant issues, use them. That is also LEAN. Changing how you document product requirements just for the sake of adopting "new approaches" is a form of waste.

Lean PRD's

However, you should investigate if there is anything else you can do to reduce waste. For example, how detailed is your PRD? Does it need to be that detailed? Does it optimally support your Lean and Agile development teams?

As a result of questions like these, many Lean teams have combined PRD's with more Agile development constructs like Backlogs and Kanban Boards (more later). Other companies have thrown out the PRD entirely or created a stripped-down version of the PRD.

The purpose of the PRD is to communicate what you are building, who it is for, and how it will benefit the end user. It also defines which product features make a Minimum Viable Product (more on that later).

If a company uses a PRD without Backlogs and/or Kanban Boards, the PRD should have goals and objectives, the Product Roadmap (sequenced Features, User Stories), assumptions, constraints, dependencies, and user interface requirements.

If a company uses any combination of PRD and other requirements repositories, the why, what, who, and how, including the Product Roadmap and Minimum Viable Product options still must be available somewhere.

Using Backlogs as Requirements Repository

Along with the Lean and Agile movement came a new concept called Backlogs. A Backlog is the newest form of a product requirements repository. It holds items that teams need to work on. Backlogs have become the repository of choice for many if not most organizations.

As with other artifacts in the Lean and Agile world, you will find all kinds of different names for Backlogs – Product Backlog, Solution Backlogs, Release Backlog, Iteration Backlogs, Sprint Backlog, Program Backlog, etc.

Some organizations, especially the ones that follow the Kanban method (a widely used Lean methodology), limit Backlogs to one Lean Product Backlog. Others, for example, development teams that follow the Scrum approach (a widely used Agile methodology) have separate Backlogs for the development teams.

Since Scrum is used extensively, we will mostly use the Scrum terminology in our example to demonstrate the use of multiple Backlogs. The three common Scrum Backlogs are:

☑ Product Backlog
☑ Release or Iteration Backlog
☑ Sprint Backlog

Product Backlog

The Product Backlog (or Backlog) is the most important one for the business community. Based on the product roadmap, the Product Backlog lists Features, Epics, User Stories, NFRs, Bug Fixes, etc. that an Agile team MAY deliver – in short, it lists all things that need to be done for the product to succeed.

Note: *The Product Backlog includes several more items that only developers need. Since this book is about Lean Business Analysis, we will not focus on them.*

A Backlog holds a set of prioritized Features and User Stories (based on the product roadmap) that are prepared and ready for the next development iteration.

It also includes unprepared items which describe what "could be done" – Features that might be developed in the future. These items can be ambiguous, unclear, incomplete, and even contradictory.

Getting Features and User Stories ready is the job of the Product Owner. This is referred to as "Backlog Management", "grooming the Backlog", or "Backlog Refinement". A Product Backlog is not set in stone. It is always in a state of flux adjusting to the changing business needs and the progress of the Agile team.

Good Product Backlog Management is critical because it can slow down or speed up development drastically. Typically, a Product Owner manages the Product Backlog either by iteration/release or continually depending on the software development methodology (more on Backlog Refinement later).

Release or Iteration Backlog

Once a Feature has been prepared and scheduled for release, User Stories associated with that Feature come out of the Product Backlog and go into a Release or Iteration Backlog.

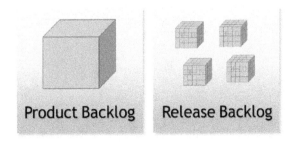

Product Backlog   **Release Backlog**

During a Release Planning Session, the team works through all items in the Release Backlog based on the Product Owner's priorities until there is a mutual understanding of the Feature(s) or User Story.

This is also the time when the team fleshes out Acceptance Criteria, often in the form of Given-When-Then Scenarios and Scenario Outlines.

Sprint Backlog

During a Sprint Planning Session, the team selects User Stories that will be coded in the upcoming Sprint from the Release Backlog. The selected items are then added to the Sprint Backlog which is updated daily by the Agile team as they move through the Sprint working towards delivering working software.

Some Scrum teams also use Kanban Boards (see next) to make the work items of the Release and Sprint Backlog more visible.

It is sometimes necessary to drill down even further into the User Stories to guarantee a mutual understanding. Business analysis techniques such as functional decomposition, workflow modeling, data modeling, and many others might be appropriate. This is, however, at the discretion of the technical team.

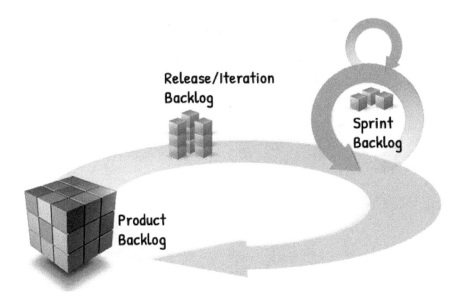

Kanban Boards

A Kanban Board is amazingly simple (which is its beauty). It has different columns that show Features, User Stories, and other work that the team is currently doing, things that the team plans to do, and things that the team has completed.

There are many variations for naming the columns (which is one of the strengths of the Kanban approach). Every organization can create the most effective Board for their success. A Kanban Board is one of the most powerful techniques for visualizing where your product is.

At the beginning, the "To-Do" column has the most items. As the team is working on them, Features, User Stories, and other items will be spread throughout various levels of analysis, development, testing, and so on. Each column represents one step in the realization of an item or task. The last column always is the "Done" column.

When you see cards (if you are using a Trello board) or Post-it notes moving across the Board you can see the progress on the project. You can also see where bottlenecks are, meaning where things get hung up.

Although the Kanban Board approach is linked to the Kanban methodology, many Scrum teams have gone to using Kanban Boards in their Release Planning meetings.

Implement		Deliver	Validate	Done
Doing	Done			

Project B   Project C   CODB   R&D

Kanban Boards are a phenomenal Release Planning tool. They are one of the primary tools of Lean development and, from a business analysis perspective, we should embrace this tool no matter what software development methodology we use.

Knowing When to Do What in a Lean and Agile World

Strategic, Tactical, and Operational Business Analysis

Due to the evolution of the external and internal environments of an organization, change is a fact of life. As a result, business analysis is an on-going activity and organizations use it at **3 major levels** of detail.

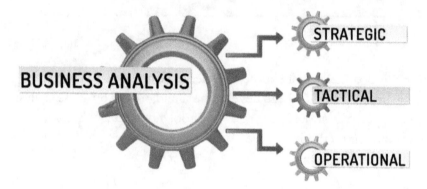

Strategic Business Analysis is the study of business visions, goals, objectives, and strategies of an organization or an organizational unit to identify the desired future. It encompasses the analysis of existing organizational structure, policies, politics, problems, opportunities, and application architecture to build a business case for change.

Strategic business analysis employs techniques such as:

- ☑ Variance Analysis
- ☑ Feasibility Analysis
- ☑ Force Field Analysis
- ☑ Decision Analysis

☑ Key Performance Indicators

to support senior management in the decision-making process. The primary outcome of this work is a set of defined, prioritized projects and initiatives that the organization will undertake to create the desired future.

If the initiative includes the development of software using an Agile Software Development Methodology (SDM), Strategic Business Analysis identifies themes and/or epics, and initiates a product backlog. For traditional methodologies, the results will be project charters and scope documents.

Tactical Business Analysis takes whatever results Strategic Business Analysis delivers to the next level of detail. This level depends on the SDM and on the relative size and complexity of the project. At the project or initiative level, it flushes out details to ensure that the evolving solution meets the needs of the business community.

At this level, business analysis:

☑ identifies impacted stakeholders

☑ captures their individual concerns

☑ elicits stakeholder requirements

☑ conducts feasibility analysis

☑ analyzes and prioritizes requirements

☑ manages changing business needs

This is the level most commonly associated with **"classic Business Analysis"** and is heavily dependent on the SDM. In a "Waterfall" project, you will put a major effort up front in defining a clear and complete set of requirements for the entire project. In Agile, you only need high-level business and stakeholder requirements at the beginning. The premise is you will drill down to sufficient levels of detail when developers are ready to start coding.

Commonly used techniques at this level include:

- ☑ Stakeholder Identification
- ☑ Interviewing
- ☑ Prioritization
- ☑ Facilitation
- ☑ Baselining
- ☑ Writing User Stories and NFR
- ☑ Coverage Matrices
- ☑ MoSCoW Analysis
- ☑ Benchmarking
- ☑ Business Rules Analysis
- ☑ Change Management
- ☑ Process and Data Modeling
- ☑ Functional Decomposition

In an Agile environment, Tactical Business Analysis adds to the Product Backlog and/or Release Plan expressed in Themes, Business Epics, Architecture Epics, User Stories, and User Story Epics.

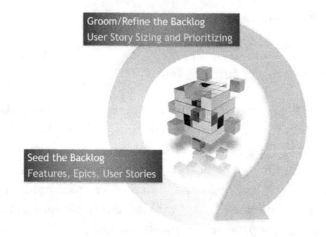

In a traditional setting, the primary outcome of Tactical Business Analysis is a set of textual and/or modeled Business and Stakeholder Requirements.

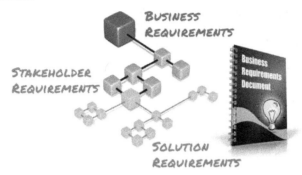

Operational Business Analysis is the third level. As input, it uses the results of Tactical Business Analysis, whether they are expressed as traditional Stakeholder Requirements or in the form of Agile Features and User Stories. It creates Solution Functional Requirements (SFR) and Non-Functional Requirements (NFR).

In traditional SDMs, this level of analysis is completed to the greatest degree possible during the Analysis phase, whereas it is recognized that some Operational Business Analysis is impossible until the design has been worked out.

In an Agile approach, business analysis expertise is needed by members of the development team who will be heavily involved in User Story elaboration and Iteration or Sprint Planning. If they are the stewards of a packaged application, they will deal primarily with identifying how to manage the application parameters to meet evolving business needs.

Their primary techniques include:

- ☑ Meeting Facilitation
- ☑ Checklist Management
- ☑ Process Mapping and Analysis
- ☑ Business Rule Analysis
- ☑ Lessons Learned Analysis
- ☑ Story Decomposition
- ☑ Test Scenario Identification
- ☑ Test Data Engineering
- ☑ Interface Analysis

All 3 Levels Share Common Elements

Few organizations staff all three levels of business analysis and even fewer use the terminology of **Strategic**, **Tactical**, and **Operational** Business Analyst. Regardless whether the individual tasked with defining a future IT solution has the title "Business Analyst" or not, someone on every project is "wearing the business analysis hat". The challenge for that individual is how can he or she get the job done?

Fundamentally, the one wearing the BA hat needs specific tools and/or techniques to do the job. To identify which are most suitable for the task, compare the results of two separate and unrelated surveys.

All three levels of business analysis share techniques such as:

- ☑ problem definition and analysis
- ☑ requirements elicitation
- ☑ requirements analysis
- ☑ requirements specification
- ☑ acceptance testing
- ☑ *and dozens of others*

As stated earlier, business analysis in the end is the business process of ensuring that the evolution of the organization mirrors the goals and objectives set by executive management.

Given that lofty purpose, it is not surprising that business analysis has become a hot topic in the global marketplace today. Organizations that recognize its importance thrive regardless of their individual choice of what to call it, who actually executes it, and when they do it. Business Analysis, under any other name, still improves an organization's probability of success.

Now let's take a closer look at the Lean life cycle.

Timing of Analysis in a Lean and Agile World

If you are working in a Lean and Agile world, Business Analysis is just as essential as it ever was. One major change, however, is the **timing** of business analysis activities.

What activities are done, when they are happening, and even how they are performed can differ significantly between a traditional and a Lean/ Agile software development life cycle.

Traditional Lifecycle

A traditional software development lifecycle (i.e. Waterfall) follows strict phases, sticking to the original requirements and design plan created at the beginning of the project.

Waterfall is a step by step process with several phases, for example, Analysis, Design, Testing, Implementation. The output of one phase becomes the input of the next phase. In short, there is no overlapping phases in a strict Waterfall model. Each phase of a Waterfall model is unique and well organized.

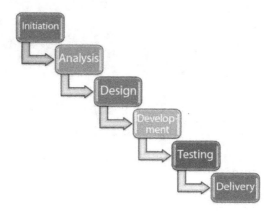

Lean and Agile Lifecycles

Agile and Lean lifecycles, on the other hand, are a set of principles that encourage flexibility, adaptability, communication and working software over plans and processes. Lean and Agile follow two important concepts – Incremental and Iterative.

Incremental product development

means building something piece by piece, like creating a picture by finishing a jigsaw puzzle.

Iterative product development

means building something through successive refinements. You start with a "minimum viable product", which is a low-pain, high-gain implementation that tests the viability and value of the product/feature. You continue by refining the product at each stage of the development process by ensuring that each new feature adds value to the customer.

Since Lean software development is incremental and iterative, Lean Business Analysis (requirements discovery and analysis) also must become incremental and iterative.

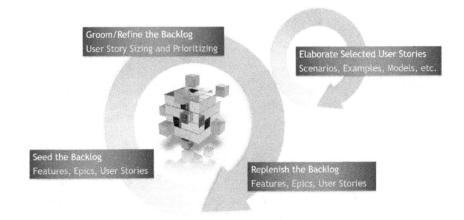

To illustrate how business analysis works in a Lean and Agile life cycle, let's look at Scrum, a widely used Agile methodology.

Scrum

To manage, seed, groom, or refine the Product Backlog (more on that later), the Agile team needs Strategic, Tactical, and Operational Business Analysis skills throughout the agile lifecycle.

At the beginning of the initiative, the team creates the Vision Statement, an initial Feature List, Epics, and high-level User Stories using **Strategic Business Analysis** skills.

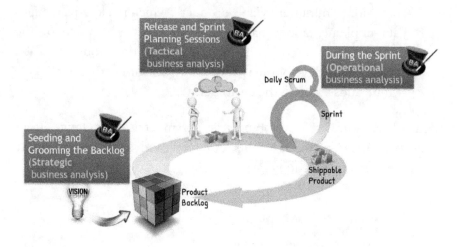

During Release (aka iteration) and Sprint Planning, the team needs **Tactical Business Analysis** skills to prepare or elaborate selected User Stories for the next release.

In the Kanban methodology, the team does not have Release Planning and Sprint Planning Sessions. Kanban teams use Cadences which are seven types of meetings. However, several of these meetings serve the same purpose as Release and Sprint Planning meetings do.

www.ingramcontent.com/pod-product-compliance
Lightning Source LLC
La Vergne TN
LVHW051241050326
832903LV00028B/2511

During the on-going development work (daily Scrums), the team applies **Operational Business Analysis** skills to drill down on Features and User Stories as needed.

As you can see, even in a Lean and Agile environment, you still need to think about Business Analysis work done at all three levels (strategic, tactical, and operational).

Seeding, Managing/Grooming the Product Backlog

Effectively managing (a.k.a. grooming/refining) Product Backlogs is critical to Lean development. Backlog Management is the on-going process by which the Product Owner (often in collaboration with a Business Analyst and/or Customer-Side Teams) adds, adjusts, prepares, and prioritizes Backlog items to make sure the technical team releases the most valuable product features to customers as soon as possible.

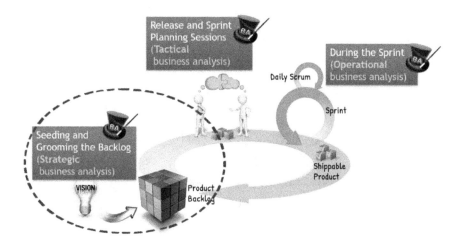

Typically, the Product Owner (or whoever manages the Backlog) is responsible for replenishing the Backlog with new Features, User Stories, etc. The Product Owner needs to right-size and refine Features, Epics, and User Stories to prioritize and estimate them properly so that the Lean/Agile team knows which feature(s) to develop in the next iteration.

Business Agility Relies on Backlog Management

What makes Lean and Agile development methods so successful is the speed of the customer feedback loop. No longer does a company have to wait years for feedback from their users and customers.

Each release takes anywhere from minutes (Continuous Delivery / Integration) to a few months (for other Lean and Agile methods). Either results in instant feedback from the user community.

However, taking advantage of this new-found knowledge depends entirely on the effectiveness of your Product Backlog Management.

Managing a Backlog is demanding since a Product Backlog is always in a state of flux adjusting to integrate new visions based upon product feedback.

It All Starts with "Seeding" the Product Backlog

Based on the Product Roadmap (high-level, strategic plan for the product), the Product Owner together with the Business Analyst, SME's, and other business-side teams add new Features, User Stories, Epics, etc. to the Backlog.

One of the most widely spread techniques for this activity are User Story Workshops (a.k.a. Story Discovery Workshops). In line with Lean principles, time spent analyzing and perfecting these "raw" User Stories while you are capturing them is a waste. You have no way of knowing which User Stories will make the cut later.

In this iteration, the goal is to describe product functionality at a level of detail sufficient to allow for a conversation between the developers and the business community.

Continuous Refinement of the Product Backlog

A Backlog requires constant grooming to remove uncertainty, identify dependencies, and avoid rework during development and testing. Typical Backlog refinement activities include:

- ☑ Adding new User Stories
- ☑ Removing outdated User Stories
- ☑ Determining User Story priority
- ☑ Estimating User Stories
- ☑ Splitting User Stories that are too large for one iteration
- ☑ ...

To prioritize User Stories, find missing functionality, and estimate effort for the next iteration, the entire Agile team needs to understand all related Stories in the Backlog in context. This is exceedingly difficult if the Stories are in a list format.

User Story Mapping

A highly recommended technique for managing Product Backlogs is User Story Mapping. This is not necessarily the same as a Product Roadmap. A Product Roadmap is a strategic product development

tool. Its purpose is to communicate the high-level overview of a product's strategy.

A Product Manager develops the Roadmap which in its simplest form is a visualization of the product's evolution. It is a tool for the Product Manager to communicate the WHY to Executives. It also serves to start a conversation with and get feedback from stakeholders.

A **User Story Map**, on the other hand, is a dynamic outline of a user's interactions with the product. The team uses a Story Map to evaluate which steps have the most benefit for the user and prioritize what should be built next. It organizes work into releases (the delivery of new customer experiences).

User Story Mapping has become an essential tool for working with Agile User Stories. During Story mapping, the team fleshers out the Product Vision into Features and User Stories by creating a User Story Map.

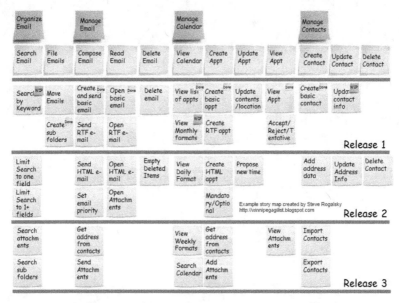

Thanks to Steve Rogalsky and the Winnipeg Agilist

In some organizations the User Story Map IS the Product Road Map. We feel that each serves a different purpose. However, as with everything in the brave new world of Lean and Agile, your organization must determine whether having both adds value or waste.

Elaborate (Prepare) User Stories for the Next Iteration

Only during Iteration Planning (or Release and Sprint Planning in Scrum), do developers need to gain a clearer understanding of detailed solution-level requirements (i.e. Functional Features and non-functional Qualities).

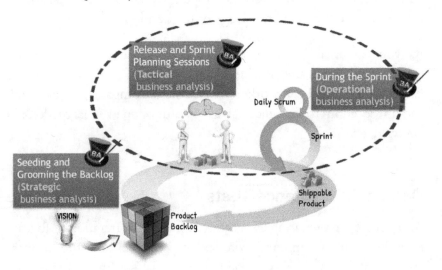

Now is the right time for developers, testers, and the business to elaborate or analyze Features and Stories that are imminent. This activity often happens during the "3-amigos conversation" which should be held when developers are ready to code.

Lean Communication and Analysis Techniques

The business team now needs effective Lean communication and requirements analysis techniques to make sure that the developers understand all aspects of the User Stories. This will allow them to create the correct functionality that the business needs.

Depending on their skill level, the developers will decide what analysis artifacts (such as functional decompositions, process diagrams, data

models, etc.) they need from the Product Owner or business-side team to ensure a mutual understanding with the business community.

Determining the Level of Detail Needed

LEAN Business Analysis also means that we no longer develop the same level of detail for every developer. We adapt the detail to the technical AND domain knowledge of the developer.

As you can imagine, a Junior Programmer will need a lot more information from the Business Analyst than a Senior Software Engineer who has been working for the same company for years and, and in addition to technical skills, has developed a large domain knowledge base.

Defining Acceptance Tests

Another step in preparing User Stories for the next Iteration or Release is fleshing out Acceptance Criteria. They express how the business community can validate the completion of a User Story. Testers use Acceptance Criteria to write and conduct their Acceptance Tests.

Organizations that subscribe to ATDD (Acceptance Test Driven Development) might already create Scenarios, Scenario Outlines and Examples. The purpose here is to enable developers and end-users to prove that the application delivers what the business community needs. We will cover more later in the chapter on "Acceptance Testing or Business-Facing Testing".

Staying One Step Ahead of the Development Team(s)

Making Business Analysis Lean means that, as Product Owner, your team must stay a step or two ahead of the development team to avoid

any waste in developers waiting for prepared and clearly defined User Stories.

However, the Agile Team only elaborates Product Backlog items (using Tactical Business Analysis techniques) for one or two releases ahead at the most. Preparing more items than needed for the next release is a violation of one of the lean principles (work should be done at "the last responsible moment").

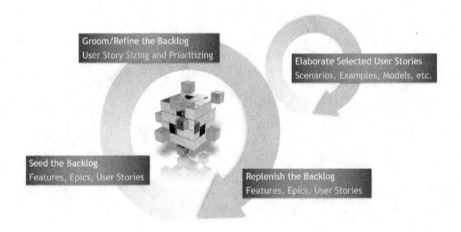

Using Feedback to Replenish the Backlog

Finally, you have finished an Iteration or Release and you have received feedback from people using your application or product on how well your new features work or are perceived to work. It is time to expand or replenish (methodologies use a different term for this task) your Product Backlog.

Reviews, Retrospectives, and Replenishment Meetings are vehicles that are used in the different approaches to refine a Backlog. This keeps the product alive and keeps it evolving as the needs evolve.

That is how Lean and Agile affect the Business Analysis process. The question now is what techniques you as "the one wearing the BA hat" can use to make sure that you are delivering LEAN requirements.

LEAN AND AGILE
BUSINESS ANALYSIS TECHNIQUES

Since every new product or project is created in response to a business need, correctly understanding those business needs is just as critical in a Lean and Agile environment as it is in traditional software development. Unfortunately, the English language is full of ambiguity and misunderstandings.

It is the responsibility of the Product Owner, the Business Analyst, or whoever is defining the business needs to make them as clear as possible to the developer community and the Stakeholders.

☑ **Developers** need to understand them to correctly code the solution

☑ **Stakeholders** need to understand them to evaluate whether the solution fits their needs

Unfortunately, you can rarely just look up business needs. You cannot apply the same methods as you would for authoring a research report. Most business or technical requirements are not documented anywhere. They exist in the minds of Stakeholders and in feedback that has yet to be obtained from end users.

This was a challenge in a traditional development environment. In today's Lean and Agile environment, we face a paradigm shift in business analysis that makes some major inroads into that.

In this chapter, we will show you a few of the most important LEAN business analysis techniques. However, there are many more available online as well as taught in classroom courses.

You can never know too much. Even after doing business analysis for the past 30 years, we (the authors) still add new tools and techniques to our BABOT[3] (Business Analysis Bag of Tips, Tricks, and Techniques) on a regular basis.

The Product Vision Statement (a.k.a. Next Big Thing)

Before any technical product development can start, the Agile team needs to understand where they are going and why.

A widely used tool to share a product's goals and purpose is the Product Vision Statement (sometimes called "the Next Big Thing"). It shows the future of the new product (or new features), what problems it will resolve, and what needs it will fulfill. It answers the WHAT, WHY, WHO, WHERE, and HOW of the product.

- ◈ **WHAT** is the business need that this product is going to fill? **WHAT** is the key benefit?
- ◈ **WHY** would it add value to the customer?
- ◈ **WHO** is the target customer? **WHO** are the competitors?
- ◈ **WHERE** does this product fit in the organizational strategy?
- ◈ **HOW** is it different than competitor products? **HOW** will it be a competitive advantage?

These are the fundamental questions that the Product Vision or "the Next Big Thing" must answer.

One of the quotes that we love from the late, great Steve Jobs is:

Steve Jobs

"If you are working on something exciting that you really care about, you don't have to be pushed.
The vision pulls you."

In our opinion. this is an extremely powerful statement. A great vision will ignite that human creativity inside of us. Keep that in mind when you write your next Product Vision.

However, if you are the Business Analyst, it is important to realize, that **creating** the Product Vision is not usually the job of the Business Analyst. It is the responsibility of the Product Owner, Product Manager, or Product Leader.

Several Lean business analysis techniques exist to use the Vision Statement as a basis in creating the Product Roadmap and getting the Product Backlog started (seeding the Backlog).

And don't forget:

KEEP IT LEAN!

A Product Vision is not static. It gets rewritten and adjusted as the team gets customer and stakeholder feedback. A Product Vision is the steppingstone to a Product Roadmap.

The Product Roadmap

The Product Roadmap is not a Lean or Agile invention. It existed long before the Lean movement. In traditional software development approaches (i.e. Waterfall), it detailed what to build for months or even years in advance of the launch.

However, like everything else, Product Roadmaps changed with the Lean movement. Many companies discovered a lot of waste in their Roadmap methods especially in the modern software development environments. Most Product Managers moved to a Lean/Agile approach for building their Roadmaps.

LEAN Product Roadmaps

Developing **Lean** Roadmaps means constantly considering product and Feature iterations based on customer feedback. In a Lean / Agile environment, a Product Roadmap is a living document that is updated when needed.

An effective Product Roadmap solves an important customer problem or offers new opportunities to customers. It does not focus on detailed Features that depict how to solve the problem or provide a new opportunity. Rather, it gives guidance on the product strategies and priorities.

Detailed Product Features belong in your Product Backlog. It is the responsibility of the Product Owner, together with a Business Analyst and/or business side teams, to define detailed Features and User Stories that will enable the technical team to build the product.

A typical Lean Product Roadmap includes:

☑ Product strategy and goals

☑ High-level product features

☑ Product feature timelines

☑ Feature responsibilities

☑ High-level priorities

A Product Roadmap should be simple and easy to understand. It should tell a coherent story about the envisioned growth of the product. It serves as the basis for another important concept in Lean and Agile software development - the Minimum Viable Product.

The Minimum Viable Product (MVP)

What is a Minimum Viable Product?

All Agile development approaches rely on iterations which are short timeboxes (usually 1-2 weeks) during which Feature development takes place. Although "Lean" approaches are not time-driven, they are still strongly focused on feature development. A valuable tool in this iterative process is the Minimum Viable Product (MVP).

The MVP is a concept that ensures that Agile teams can iterate product development intelligently. The MVP allows the team to develop just enough Features to satisfy early customers and get quick feedback for future product development. The team can then validate a product idea early and improve on it.

When Steve Jobs started the iPhone development, he had no idea of the end goal. The iPhone became a hugely successful product because of customer feedback and iteration development. It got out into

people's hands and they told him what they liked, what they did not like, and it evolved from there.

The idea behind Lean and Agile development is not to plan everything out to the nth degree but to go with the flow. As you get feedback you improve the product.

Once you have a product that people are using, you can think about adding new Minimum Viable Features (a.k.a. Minimum Buyable Features). The whole idea is to grow the product quickly and delight your customers with new Features on a regular basis.

How Do You Define an MVP?

The concept of a Minimum Viable Product originated in the Lean Startup movement. Eric Ries, the author of "The Lean Startup" defined an MVP as:

> "... that version of a new product which allows a team to collect the maximum amount of validated learning about customers with the least effort."

Seems pretty clear. As always, the devil is in the detail and defining a successful MVP that allows your business to quickly reevaluate and improve your product is not trivial.

When defining a Minimum Viable Product, a good place to start is by focusing on solving a problem for one persona. Make sure that the persona you pick is representative of many of your customers. An MVP should not deliver functionality that only a few people would like.

Determine the Must-Haves AND Exciting Perks

Next, determine the basic needs (not the wants) of that persona and then add some exciting perks. You want people to be eager to try your new product to get the feedback you need. It is ok to leave some Product Features incomplete if they are only nice-to-haves. However, do not skimp on the must-haves.

An MVP is not necessarily a marketable product. You might need to add more Minimum Viable Features before you can release the product. As Elijah Chang writes,

> "Releasing your MVP doesn't mean that you will be ready to go to market and launch to the world. You'll likely need to iterate for a little bit and find that critical mass of features that have been tested, validated, and used. You may find that you need a couple of MVPs combined before you're ready to go to market. The point at which you're ready to launch is called the Minimum Marketable Product (MMP)."

This will become an endless cycle of evaluating customer feedback and determining Minimum Viable Features for the next release. In the new world of Lean software development, there will never be a last version of your product.

We have come a lot closer to true business agility and achieved a long-held dream of the business community, namely quickly make major changes to existing products and release new features.

Lean Requirements Communication Techniques

The major advantage of all Lean and Agile philosophies is speed and agility. Therefore, in an Agile environment, business communication must be fast and flexible. Conversations between technical and business-side teams are at the heart of Lean development approaches.

All Agile team members need effective communication skills to define and elaborate Features, User Stories, functional requirements, etc. as the product progresses.

These skills are critical at various stages, for example, while seeding and grooming the Product Backlog, during Release and Iteration Planning, and during other conversations between developers and end-users, just to name a few.

Whether you have a conversation with an end-user, a formal "Requirements Meeting" with the sales team, or a "Requirements Discovery Workshop" with the Agile Team, you should always be prepared to avoid wasting anyone's time (including your own).

Preparing to be a Lean BA

For every conversation you should:

→ Prepare the right questions

→ Find the right people (stakeholders)

→ Clearly communicate the goals of the conversation

→ Manage the logistics of the conversation

→ Determine the right level of detail

→ Plan how to capture the responses

→ Decide how to use visual representations

Prepare Questions, People (Stakeholders), and Goals

To prepare the right questions, you need to make sure that you understand enough about the product and your stakeholders to be able to ask the right questions. If you ask a salesclerk about the long-term strategy of your organization or their department, they might have an opinion, but it may or may not be shared by the executive level.

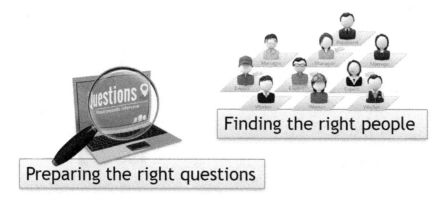

Finding the right people

Preparing the right questions

Since working with the right people at the right time is crucial to Lean, you need stakeholder identification techniques for finding them.

To make sure that you are avoiding waste, you should also clearly communicate the goals of the conversation and be able to defend to anyone why the team needs this conversation now.

Prepare and Manage Logistics

Furthermore, you must manage the logistics of any meeting. For example, the Three Amigo conversation is a widely used type of meeting where developer(s), tester(s), the Product Owner, and a business expert elaborate on Features, Epics, and User Stories.

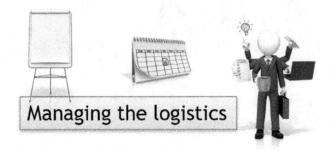

If it is a larger Three Amigos conversation (strangely enough, you can have a lot more than three people participating), you will need to plan for a room, tables, chairs, flip chart, audio/video equipment, maybe even catering and refreshment, etc.

Determine Level of Detail

Next, decide what level of detail the team needs to work out during the conversation. For instance, if it is a Sprint or Iteration Planning meeting, you might need to drill down to the functional and acceptance test level.

On the other hand, during a Requirements Discovery Workshop, you are looking for high-level Features, Epics, and User Stories to fill your Product Backlog.

Determine How to Capture Responses

Since you are getting valuable information from the technical and business teams, you also must decide how to capture the responses. Consider using a recording, flip chart, white board, any electronic means, or cocktail napkins - whatever works.

Deciding how to capture the responses

Decide on Visual Models

You also might consider **drawing diagrams or pictures**. Now, in the Lean and Agile world, we rarely draw a model of the entire product.

Lean conversations focus on outcomes that the team or someone on the team needs very soon. Full Process Models seem like overkill and a lot of wasted time. This does, however, not change the fact that pictures are still much more powerful at communicating than mere words.

For example, if a team tries to form a mutual understanding on a Feature for a complex workflow, ask yourself what picture or diagram fragment would help the participants better understand or express their needs.

Being Prepared is LEAN

Although it seems that all of this is a lot of preparation and could be a waste of your time, these tasks are part of doing Lean Business Analysis.

You are making sure that you are doing things in the most effective way. Being prepared for conversations, wills save others a lot of time and

SAVING EFFORT IS NOT ABOUT ONE PERSON BUT ABOUT THE WHOLE TEAM.

Picking the Right Mode of Communication

In today's world, we have many different modes of communication available to us. From in-person conversations to email, instant messaging, teleconferencing, video conferencing, and group interactions like a formal workshop, there seem to be endless possibilities to talk to each other.

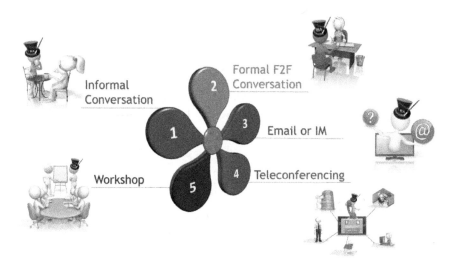

Especially in a Lean and Agile environment, you should take advantage of the different modes of conversations and evaluate which serves your purpose better. However, this requires careful choices because a lot of wasted time can hide in these different conversational modes. In Lean Business Analysis, even your conversations should follow the Lean principles.

One-on-one Conversations

For example, you can choose an **informal conversation** where you happen to meet someone accidentally. You might be walking down the hall and bump into somebody that you have been trying to contact for a couple of days. Just make sure that you have a set of prepared questions always with you.

You can also schedule a **formal face-to-face conversation**. In this case both of you have time to prepare for the meeting.

Exchanging **e-mail or instant messaging (IM)** are popular modes especially if the only thing you want to ask is a quick, clarifying question. Limit this mode of communication to brief questions and answers.

Video- and Teleconferencing

If your organization is spread around the globe, you will likely never have the luxury of getting together in person. That is where you need teleconferences or online / virtual meetings.

Some people believe that the idea of sitting through a requirement meeting via teleconference seems like torture. It can be if it is poorly facilitated. However, online meetings have their advantages. For example, it is much easier to share all kinds of documents in an online meeting and even annotate them.

Facilitated Workshops

Finally, Requirements Workshops or User Story Workshops are common in getting an Agile Initiative started or replenishing a Product Backlog. The workshop is an excellent tool to deliver first-cut User Stories or Features to seed the Product Backlog.

It allows groups to think about a common need and express Features and User Story candidates by feeding off each other's thoughts. If you are looking for innovative solutions and features, a Workshop is your best bet.

User Story or Requirements Workshops can be virtual or face-to-face, however, the virtual workshop needs an experienced online facilitator. To improve your odds of success, add an in-session Business Analyst.

Managing Risk Alleviates Uncertainty

The Cynefin Framework

There is a new sheriff in town called Cynefin (kun-EF-in) which is a Welsh word meaning something like "belonging to", or "habitat".

Dave Snowden developed this technique at the beginning of this century and described it as "making sense of complexity in order to act".

Cynefin is a great tool to prioritize and analyze business problems, Features, User Stories, and other requirement types. It is a decision-support framework that can increase the probability of making the right decision in any situation.

Minimize Risk by Decreasing Uncertainty

One of the biggest problems facing any new undertaking is uncertainty. Uncertainty exists everywhere. At the beginning of a new initiative, at best you have a faint idea of what it is supposed to accomplish.

Especially in Lean and Agile environments, new Features or User Stories often are not detailed enough to give us a clear picture, meaning there is a high degree of uncertainty.

The purpose of Cynefin is to help us quickly assess a new situation and decide how to best handle it. In terms of Lean Business Analysis, it is a way of minimizing risk. It guides us in the early stages of an initiative or project when we are dealing with a lot of uncertainty.

There are **4 different decision-making domains**:

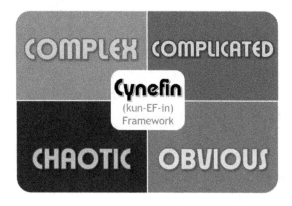

In each of the domains, you should use a different approach.

The **OBVIOUS** Domain

The OBVIOUS (aka: SIMPLE) domain is for simple tasks, problems, requirements, etc. If you know exactly how to handle a situation, or you have a set of instructions that you can follow, then it is just a question of getting the job done.

This domain is characterized by the fact that you at least think you are dealing with "**Known-Knowns**" (which may or may not be true!).

The COMPLICATED Domain

If you know what to do but there are many different variables that can come into play for your solution, you are in the COMPLICATED domain.

A common situation that puts you in this domain is that you are doing something your team has never done before or at least never in this environment.

This domain usually requires some analysis. According to Snowden, items in this domain are situations where:

- ☑ you think you know what you need to know

- ☑ you know what questions to ask or you know that there are people whom you can ask - people who have been there and done that

In this domain, you deal primarily with **Known-Unknowns**.

The OBVIOUS as well as the COMPLICATED domain are ordered, meaning cause and effect are known or can be discovered.

An Example of OBVIOUS and COMPLICATED

Many business analysis tasks fall in these two domains. For example, assuming your team has worked with secure logins on websites, an OBVIOUS User Story would be:

"As Account Holder, I can log into my bank account to see my latest transactions"

An example for the COMPLICATED domain could be:

"As office manager, I want to determine the most profitable daily and weekly rates for our hotel rooms"

In this case, the office manager has step by step instructions on how to calculate the most profitable room rate. However, room prices change based on many factors such as what competitors are charging, the time of year, local events, target occupancy, minimum acceptable occupancy, and many others.

This User Story might even be an Epic based on the large number of variables that have to be considered. That is not a problem assuming that you have the right business analysis techniques to split this Epic into User Stories that fall into the OBVIOUS domain.

The COMPLEX Domain

Complexity is a daunting challenge. Some Epics, Problems, Goals, User Stories, Features, etc. fall into the **COMPLEX** domain. This domain is on the "unordered" side of the equation, meaning cause and effect are not only unknown but potentially unknowable.

We are in this domain if we do not even know if anybody has ever done anything like it. This is the domain where analysis fails us. We do not really know what questions to ask and whom we could ask for help.

If any part of a User Story, Epic, Feature, etc. falls into the complex domain, life just got a whole lot more exciting. The only thing that you can do here is trying to develop "safe to fail" experiments. Try stuff out and see what works. Just make sure that if it does not work, it will not make the situation worse. That is the "safe" part of "safe to fail".

If you find something that improves the situation, you can move that part of the item over into the complicated domain. There, you can collaborate with other people to work out a satisfactory solution.

The CHAOS Domain

The final domain in Cynefin is CHAOS. Here, you have no idea what the problem is AND no idea what caused it. You really have no idea what to do. The primary difference between COMPLEX and CHAOTIC is timing. In a chaotic situation. you must react because things are falling apart.

An example of a situations that you might face in a chaotic world is your organization's primary production system failing.

- ⊠ It does not work
- ⊠ You cannot get it working again and you do not know why
- ⊠ Going to a backup does not work either because you would lose irreplaceable production data

Minimize the Damage

Chaotic situations require immediate action to minimize the damage. There is no time to develop "safe to fail" because the situation is

deteriorating second by second. Your system is dying. You need to do something at once.

In these situations, the only recommendation is do something, anything, and see if it made things better. Once you have found a partial solution that at least made a positive difference, expand it. Keep improving it until the situation stabilizes and then you can start to think about those "safe to fail" solutions.

Assessing the Complexity of Features, Epics, and User Stories

Cynefin is a powerful tool that many organizations use in assessing the relative complexity of User Stories, Epics, Features, Business Problems or Pain-Points, etc. It is extremely valuable because it is relative. The relative complexity of any item depends on the knowledge and skills of the Agile team.

The major risk in Cynefin is misjudging the relative complexity of the situation. Too many people only see one dimension of a problem and are quick to suggest a simple solution. Implementing a simple solution that has unintended consequences can quickly tip the system from any domain into CHAOS.

What Makes Cynefin Lean?

Cynefin is Lean in that it helps you recognize the potential for wasted effort before you start. If you accurately assess the relative complexity, you do not waste time trying to analyze a COMPLICATED or OBVIOUS situation but focus instead on "safe-to-fail" tests for items in the COMPLEX domain **first**. On the other hand, you do not have to waste your time in costly trials and errors in a situation that has an obvious solution.

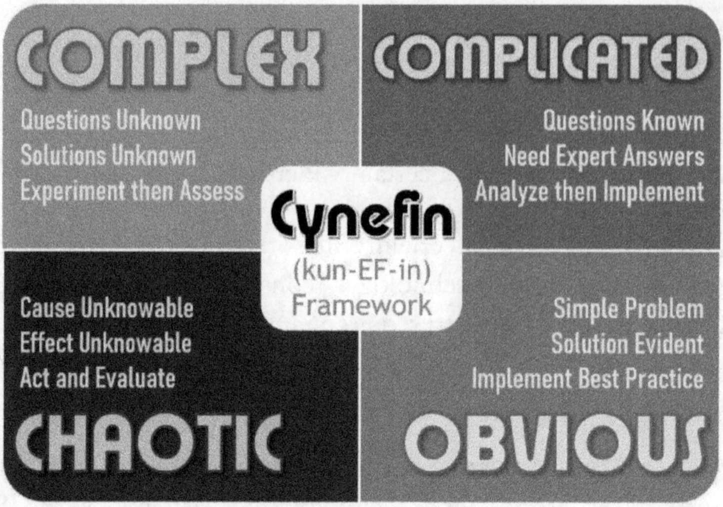

COMPLEX

Questions Unknown
Solutions Unknown
Experiment then Assess

COMPLICATED

Questions Known
Need Expert Answers
Analyze then Implement

Cynefin
(kun-EF-in)
Framework

Cause Unknowable
Effect Unknowable
Act and Evaluate

Simple Problem
Solution Evident
Implement Best Practice

CHAOTIC

OBVIOUS

The Stacey Matrix

Trying to assess the relative complexity of a software solution is so challenging that we need all the help we can get. Complexity rises (IMHO exponentially) as uncertainty increases.

The major sources of uncertainty in software development are the current state of the technology (constantly evolving) and the confidence that the captured requirements are right.

A great tool for evaluating the complexity of goals, requirements, Features, User Stories, and technological feasibility is the Stacey Matrix. Ralph Stacey created this phenomenal guide to help managers and leaders evaluate potential decision-making and best management actions.

It builds on Cynefin by selecting any 2 assessable dimensions (i.e. Requirements/Technology, Budget/Schedule, Data/Processes, etc.) that in combination will help you determine the relative complexity. It is a versatile tool in that you can quickly contrast any two related dimensions of a situation.

Stacey Matrix Adapted to Software Development

The following is an example of using the Stacey Matrix as an adjunct to Cynefin that allows you to visualize complexity. Although Stacey did not design it specifically for software development, it fits exceptionally well.

The adapted Stacey Matrix helps you to identify the Cynefin domain (relative complexity) of a Feature, User Story, Problem, etc. by assessing the existing **agreement on the requirements** AND the **technological uncertainty of the item.**

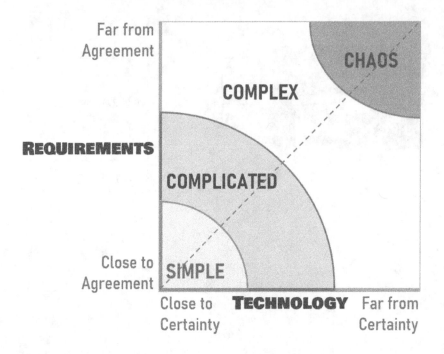

The chart above visualizes that SIMPLE digital solutions require known technology and requirements that everyone agrees on. The farther away you get on either dimension (Technology and/or Requirements) the higher the complexity.

For example, if you have no agreement on the requirements (or User Stories) AND the technology is very unclear or uncertain, you are looking at CHAOS as expressed in Cynefin terminology.

Now all you need to do is figure out how much agreement on the requirements there is amongst all stakeholders AND how stable the technology platform is.

WITH THE ADDITION OF THE STACEY MATRIX, CYNEFIN BECOMES SIMPLE, RIGHT?

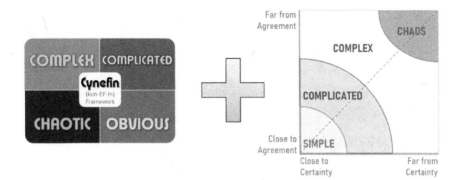

Pain-Point Analysis Reveals Your MVP, Potential Features, and User Stories

To succeed in today's fast-moving environment, organizations must be able to respond rapidly to customer feedback. This starts with recognizing problems that customers are experiencing and follows with quickly releasing new products or Features to solve them.

Successful products focus on customer Pain-Points and deliver solutions to ease those pains. Marketing has used this pearl of wisdom for a long time. But how does this concept apply to Lean Business Analysis?

Since a Pain-Point is a problem that customers of your business are experiencing, finding and analyzing those customer Pain-Points leads to better Minimum Viable Products, Features, User Stories, and other requirements.

Having well-defined customer Pain-Points enables Lean and Agile teams to ideate and explore potential solutions. A key skillset to achieving this level of clarity is Pain-Point or Problem Analysis.

Pain-Point Analysis
for Business Needs Elicitation

If you do not investigate the cause of the problem or customer Pain-Point, you can easily define a Minimum Viable Product or develop Features and User Stories that you think are spectacular only to discover that you did not solve the problem. Your solution might even make matters worse!

There is another reason we recommend using Pain-Point Analysis to find Epics, Features, and User Stories. There are optimists and pessimists everywhere. Some people view the "glass half-empty", others "half-full" meaning they either prefer positive or negative thinking. It is safe to assume that some of your Stakeholders are "glass half-empty" kind of folks and others think in "glass half-full" terms.

In our experience, if you ask a person who leans toward **negative** thinking what they want the new application or product to do, you will get a blank stare and maybe a few answers if you are lucky. They do not think in those terms. However, if you ask them what their problems are, you will get a huge list. Analyzing those Pain-Points will lead you to excellent User Stories, Features, and other requirements.

We hope we have convinced you of the huge benefits of Pain-Point analysis. Next, we will describe a few widely used techniques.

Agile and Lean
Pain-Point Analysis Techniques

The expected result / goal of any pain-point analysis technique is to discover the root cause or "real problem". Trying to fix symptoms instead of the "real" problem is sometimes tempting. However, it can be dangerous. You spend time, money, and resources making the pain go away only to realize that the underlying problem is still there causing new symptoms.

If you know the cause of a problem then you can focus User Story discovery, Minimum Viable Product definition, and other requirements elicitation efforts on solving the "real problem" instead of its associated symptoms.

Root Cause Analysis

The most widely used paint point analysis technique is Root Cause Analysis (RCA). RCA helps pinpoint contributing factors to a problem or event. The technique assumes that everything is interrelated. An action in one area triggers a chain reaction that can be anywhere from unsettling to catastrophic. By tracing the chain backwards, you can discover where the problem started and how it grew into the symptoms you are now facing. The closer to the source you can avoid the problem, the better.

Fishbone Diagram (Ishikawa Diagram)

Another method is cause and effect analysis. A Fishbone Diagram (Ishikawa Diagram) sorts probable causes into various categories that branch off from the original problem. It is a visual representation of cause and effect.

Example of a Fishbone Diagram:

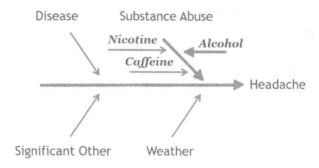

The 5 Whys

A widely used Agile paint point analysis technique is "The 5 Whys". By repeatedly asking a "Why" question, you can peel away the layers of symptoms which can lead to the root cause of a problem. You do not need to limit yourself to five questions; that is just a rule of thumb.

The 5 Whys technique was first introduced by Sakichi Toyoda, the founder of Toyota Motor Corporation. It is a lean/agile technique for simple problems, it is not particularly useful for complex problems or a large list of problems.

Problem/Symptom Reduction

The pain-point analysis technique that has worked best for us is a modified Problem/Symptom Reduction (PSR). In addition to discovering the root cause or "real problem", this problems analysis technique identifies as a by-product potential Lean requirements or business needs.

PSR is a 4-step root cause analysis technique focusing on finding the REAL problem that a customer, consumer, or stakeholder has. It was first introduced by Don Gauss and Jerry Weinberg in the 80's. Since it is our favorite technique, we will go into a little more detail.

Problem/Symptom Reduction (PSR)

Compile a Business Problem List

PSR starts by asking all stakeholders what problems they perceive that a proposed change should solve. Once you have compiled a list of all the problems that your Stakeholders perceive, you are ready for the next step.

Whose Problem Is It?

In the next step, you want to figure out WHOSE problem it is. For each problem, ask questions such as,

- ◇ Who suffers because of this problem?
- ◇ Who can affect the problem?
- ◇ Who cares how you solve the problem?
- ◇ Who does **not** want to solve the problem?

This will show you the players you need to involve to accurately analyze the problem. As a by-product, this will also confirm or complete your list of stakeholders.

Can We Solve the Problem?

In the third step, ask the question whether anyone on the Lean / Agile team or amongst the Stakeholders has the authority and the knowledge to fix this problem or Pain-Point?

If you find an item on the list where you realize that no Stakeholder has the authority or means, to do anything about it, mark this problem "Out of Scope", take it off the problem list, or add it to an OOS Problem List (someone else might be able to solve this Pain-Point).

At this time, you know the stakeholders and you have cut problems that are out of scope from your list, the rest of the items are either real problems, symptoms of real problems, or potential solutions.

Identify Potential Solutions

Problems and symptoms are easy to understand. If you have a headache, you take aspirin. That will address the symptom. But the underlying cause of your headache might be as serious as a tumor or just a night on the town.

But what are potential solutions? Potential Solutions show **one way** of solving a Pain-Point or problem. They are a welcome addition to our list of preliminary requirements that will later lead us to User Stories, Epics, Features, Scenarios, etc. But we want to remove them from our

problem list which will make it easier to separate the "real problems" from the symptoms in our last step.

Is the Problem a Symptom of Another Problem?

You have gone through the problem list twice. You have removed "problems" that were out of scope and you have removed "problems" that were solutions in disguise (or potential requirements). This is the last time you will go through this list and, yes, finally, you get to identify the "real problems".

This time, for each remaining problem on your list, ask your Stakeholders,

> *"Assuming we could solve this problem, would any of the other problems on the list go away?"*

Compare each statement on the list with every other statement.

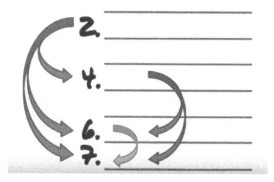

At a later stage, you define User Stories, Features, or requirements for solving these "real problems" or "causes" and all related symptoms should disappear (if they don't you are missing requirements).

To summarize,

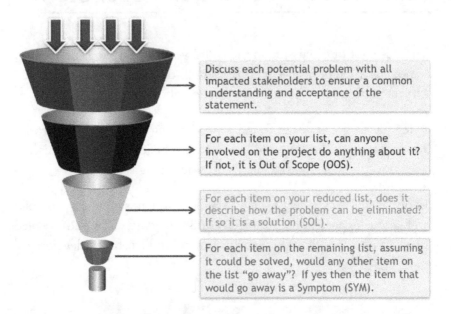

Discuss each potential problem with all impacted stakeholders to ensure a common understanding and acceptance of the statement.

For each item on your list, can anyone involved on the project do anything about it? If not, it is Out of Scope (OOS).

For each item on your reduced list, does it describe how the problem can be eliminated? If so it is a solution (SOL).

For each item on the remaining list, assuming it could be solved, would any other item on the list "go away"? If yes then the item that would go away is a Symptom (SYM).

We have used this technique on hundreds of projects and initiatives over the years. To give you an example, on one project we assembled a problem list of 105 problem statements in response to the question, "What is wrong with your current process?".

After we applied Lean Problem Symptom Reduction, we ended up with 3 real problems. Everything else was either a symptom, a solution, or a problem that was out of scope.

You can really simplify a list of perceived problems very quickly with this approach and get a head start on defining an MVP that will delight your customers or discover potential Features, Epics, and User Stories to seed your Product Backlog.

Ambiguity in Features and User Stories

There is a lot of discussion in the Agile world that there is no need to remove ambiguity from User Stories until the developers, testers, and subject matter exerts have a conversation about the Story.

A few days ago, we even found a post stating "the best User Stories are not written, they are told". We do not believe in this premise. It does not follow Lean principles. Why you might ask?

In our opinion, even in a Lean and Agile world, it is quite easy to build ambiguous expectations. Ambiguity and subjectivity still lead to failed Product Features, disappointed customers, and frustrated developers.

The Need for a Mutual Understanding

A mutual understanding of a User Story or Feature within the Lean / Agile team is critical to a successful implementation. Anyone, from the author of a User Story to the business community, the technical team, and the testers who prove whether the User Story is working correctly, must be on the same page. Any ambiguity and/or subjectivity in a User Story endangers this understanding.

Sure, following the principles of Lean Business Analysis, you do not want to waste time removing ambiguity and subjectivity while you are seeding a Product Backlog or creating a Feature List. At that time, you have no idea if these User Stories or Features will ever make it to a future release.

REMOVING AMBIGUITY AT THAT POINT WOULD BE AGAINST LEAN PRINCIPLES.

However, when you get your User Stories ready for Release Planning or Sprint Planning, that is the right time to reduce or even eliminate ambiguity and subjectivity - just before the programmers start to code.

In Lean methodologies such as Kanban, the Replenishment Meeting (one of the cadences) is like Release Planning in Scrum. During this meeting, items from the Product Backlog are pulled onto the Kanban

Board. That is the time that you want to remove any ambiguity or subjectivity.

Yes, this is an extra effort, but it follows Lean principles because it adds value AND can save a lot of time during conversations with developers, testers, and business-side teams if your User Stories have as little ambiguity and subjectivity as possible.

Imagine, the product owner, together with a SME or end-users, would clean up ambiguous User Stories when they prepare them for the next iteration? The result? The development team would not waste time trying to understand and negotiate ambiguous words and phrases.

What Exactly Is Ambiguity and Subjectivity?

There is a significant difference between ambiguity and subjectivity. Ambiguity is a statement, word, or phrase that is open to multiple legitimate interpretations. The only way that you can resolve ambiguity is by putting the statement in context.

For example, if I say: "I saw her duck". You do not know whether she is ducking or whether she has a duck.

I saw her duck!

Add Context to Remove Ambiguity

The best way to resolve ambiguity is **context**. If we were talking about pets, you would have a much better idea as to which of those two we meant.

In the world of User Stories, if you clearly define the business value and the role (or WHO) of your User Story, you are adding valuable context.

Objectify to Remove Subjectivity

Subjectivity, on the other hand, is something that is based upon a personal interpretation, your feelings, taste, or opinion. The best way to resolve subjectivity effectively is by objectifying it. Take out the abstract and make it something concrete.

For example, instead of saying:

"As an inventory control manager, I need accurate DATA to anticipate short-comings."

---

write:

"As an inventory control manager, I need accurate SALES PREDICTIONS to anticipate short-comings."

And you still could make "accurate" more concrete.

Removing Ambiguity and Subjectivity with INVEST

One approach to removing ambiguity and subjectivity is the **INVEST** method. This technique makes it easy to add context and concrete examples to a User Story. INVEST is a tool for remembering six characteristics that a good User Story has.

Independent means that each User Story should be self-contained to avoid dependencies on other User Stories. A Story that is independent of any other Story needs less context to be clear which makes it less ambiguous.

Negotiable is a key criterion in Lean and Agile development environments. To support this, a User Story should never be so detailed or restrictive that it prevents the Agile team from arriving at the best solution. Capturing clear and non-ambiguous intentions but leaving enough room for team discussion is definitively a challenge.

Valuable gives you a way to add context. If the business value is clear, the User Story is easier to understand and therefore less ambiguous.

Estimating the size of a Story is something that the developers need to do. Every User Story must have enough information to make a reasonable estimate of the Story's complexity. Removing ambiguity by adding context, will enable the Agile team to quickly estimate the Story effort during Release Planning.

Small in this context means it is at a size that a developer can code within a few days or a single Sprint at the most. It should never take more than two weeks to complete the coding of a Story.

And finally, the T stands for **Testable**. In Lean/Agile approaches, we have finally recognized that Test Scenarios or Acceptance Criteria **ARE** the real requirements that IT needs. They are the best tool to remove subjectivity. Scenarios and other forms of Acceptance Criteria are concrete examples of User Story outcomes.

Drilling Down on Epics, Features, User Stories, and Requirements

Right-sized Stories and Solution-level Requirements

During Backlog Grooming or Refinement, the Lean Business Analyst, Requirements Analyst, Product Owner, or Subject Matter Expert together with the developers drill down and right-size Epics, Features, and User Stories to make sure that the developers can discuss and understand all aspects of the User Stories. This will allow them to create the correct functionality that the business needs.

However, during Iteration Planning (Release / Sprint Planning), developers need a clear understanding of **solution-level requirements** (i.e. Functional Features and non-functional Qualities). Therefore, the Agile team needs to drill down even further into Features and User Stories.

There are several lean drill-down techniques that will make your life as a "Lean Business Analyst" a lot easier.

User Story Splitting

The most well-known technique is User Story Splitting (Story splitting for short). Exceptionally large User Stories are known as Epics. Whether the Story is considered an Epic or just too large for a single Release, the team needs to break it down into multiple, implementable User Stories.

You can split Stories while refining the Product Backlog or, at the latest, in preparation for a Sprint or coding.

User Story Splitting is a critical skill for every Agile team. However, any User Story author will benefit from knowing how to make User Stories smaller.

Story Splitting Is a Collaborative Effort

If you rely exclusively on the Product Owner to split all User Stories, you might find that the new Stories are not always split in a useful way. You need the input of the business community and the developer community. To be effective, Story splitting should be a collaborative effort. Everyone needs to work together on "intelligent" splitting.

Here is an example of a User Story split from one of our Case Studies.

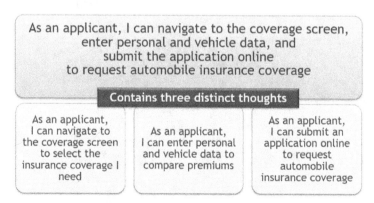

There are many Story splitting techniques that you can find online.

Functional Feature Drill-down and Story Decomp

Sometimes, for example during the current iteration, a User Story must be broken down into functional items so that it can be coded. We worked on several products where Agile developers preferred Sprint Backlogs that had User Stories broken down to Functional Features.

Story Decomp or Feature Drill-down is a technique that system analysts and designers used in Waterfall as a tool to make design decisions. At the beginning of the project they defined Functional and Non-functional Requirements for the entire scope of the project. Obviously, the timing is different in a Lean environment.

Lean practices require that you make design decisions at the last responsible moment. You should not define functional items for User Stories that are still in the Product Backlog.

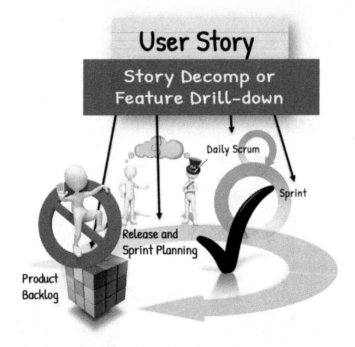

We cannot expand on the topic in this book. If you want to learn more, read our book on functional decomposition (you can find it on Amazon: "Functional and Non-Functional Requirements – Simple Requirements Decomposition / Drill-Down Techniques for Defining IT Application Behaviors and Qualities")

Decision Tables

Decision Tables are a simpler solution than Cynefin and the Stacey Matrix to reduce complexity and uncertainty in User Stories, Features, or requirements. They are excellent tools to express complex business rules that require combinations of conditions.

Decision Tables make the deliberation of Acceptance Criteria and Given-When-Then Scenarios a snap. For example, using the Decision Table below, it is easy to identify critical Scenarios or Scenario Outlines for Acceptance Testing. They are right there in front of you.

Each column in a Decision Table is at least ONE Scenario!

Conditions							
New Debt > 4X Gross Income	Y	Y	Y	N	N	N	N
Job Exp. > 5 Years	Y		N	Y	Y	N	N
Credit Excellent	Y	N		Y	N	Y	N
Credit Good				Y			
Outcomes							
Approve Loan	✓			✓	✓	✓	
Request Co-Signer	✓				✓		
Deny		✓	✓				✓

We will discuss Acceptance Testing, Scenarios and Outlines in more detail in the next chapter.

Lean Use Cases

For many developers, Use Cases are the preferred tool for drilling down to the functional requirements of a product **in preparation for a Sprint or coding**. A Use Case describes interactions between a user and software.

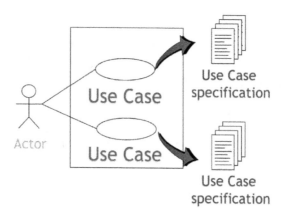

Just like with Decision Tables, Use Cases are an excellent tool to quickly create GIVEN-WHEN-THEN Scenarios that are needed for Acceptance / Business-Facing Testing.

Use Case Scenarios vs GIVEN-WHEN-THEN Scenarios

A word of caution; Use Cases also can have scenarios and it is easy to mix up the definitions of "GIVEN-WHEN-THEN Scenarios" (which are Test Scenarios) and "Use Case Scenarios". A Use Case Scenario is a single path through a Use Case and can be converted easily into a GIVEN-WHEN-THEN Scenario.

Just-In-Time LEAN Use Cases

In a Lean and Agile environment, the timing and purpose of Use Cases have changed. We no longer create a thundering herd of Use Cases to demonstrate the functionality of an entire product or application in its end form. We build just enough LEAN Use Cases to explain the next Feature or set of User Stories to our technical team.

Developing, Presenting, and Analyzing Visual Models

Sometimes words are just not enough to communicate effectively. That is when you need to pull another business analysis technique out of your bag.

Visual models, such as Process, Object, or Data Models show workflow or information usage. They will help the Subject Matter Expert (SME) recognize bottlenecks, problem areas, and find requirements and Features for improvement.

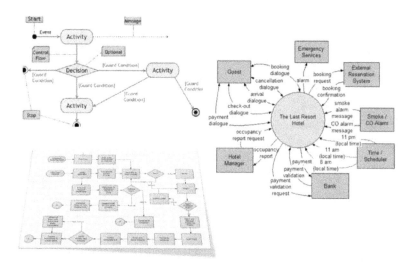

The visual models help a good analyst better understand why people are doing what they are doing, and how important it is to keep a certain workflow.

Many times, when we have helped SME's visualize their workflow, they found areas they could improve by simply changing the sequence of process steps or by changing how they did things.

The more modeling conventions you know, the better equipped you are to quickly throw up a picture that helps everyone focus on specific aspects of a process.

Generic Process Models and Dataflow Diagrams

Different models show specific aspects, and in support of Lean and Agile principles, keep your models simple. Just make sure the model expresses the essence of what you want to communicate and do not capture unnecessary information.

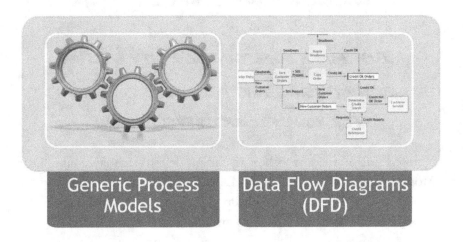

Generic Process Models

Data Flow Diagrams (DFD)

You can use generic process models, or you can use things like Data Flow Diagrams (DFD's) if you want to depict or understand the creation, consumption, transportation, and storage of data.

UML Diagrams, BPMN Models, Data Models, and Object Models

You can use Activity Diagrams (UML diagram) to show the sequence in which events are happening. Or, if you want to go into some serious process modeling because you need to reengineer some business processes, the Business Process Modeling Notation is your best bet.

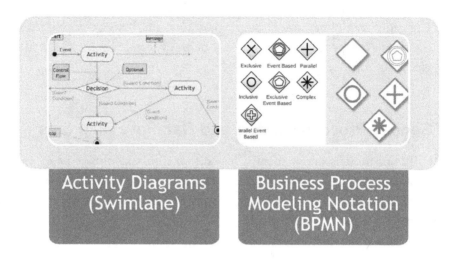

Activity Diagrams (Swimlane)

Business Process Modeling Notation (BPMN)

JUST MAKE SURE THAT YOU STAY LEAN

AND THAT USING THIS TECHNIQUE IS JUSTIFIED

FOR YOUR PRODUCT DEVELOPMENT.

You can also use any other visual modeling technique like Data Models, Object Models, and UML diagrams. Anything that works for your situation. The idea is to keep it simple but detailed enough for your developers to clearly understand the business need.

Acceptance or Business-Facing Testing

ATDD and BDD

A new testing paradigm has evolved with Lean and Agile software development. ATDD (Acceptance Test-Driven Development) and/or BDD (Behavior-Driven Development) are a major shift in thinking from earlier development methodologies in that they require the business team or test engineers to develop Acceptance Tests **before** developers create the application.

In ATDD and BDD, a domain expert (SME, Product Owner, Project Manager, Line Manager, Test Engineer, etc.) with developer guidance (if needed) starts off with "writing a User Story, Feature, or requirement statement" and then "writes as many failing Acceptance Tests" as that User Story or Feature needs.

The developers take one Scenario and "Write (lower level) Failing Unit Tests". They then repeat the Test-Driven Development cycle (Write Failing Unit Test, Make Unit Test Pass, Refactor Code, etc.) until all their Unit Tests have passed. This unit is then promoted to the next test level, typically integration or system testing, and the same tests are executed as part of those more expansive test suites.

Once they have proven that their code passes all unit, integration, system, etc. Tests, the Acceptance Test or Scenario comes back for domain expert testing ("Make Acceptance Test Pass"). If accepted by the domain expert, the developers integrate that code into the application.

This is known in geek-speak as "Refactoring" and as the ones wearing the BA hat, we do not need to know anything else about this topic. The last step in this cycle is "Sign-Off" and then we tackle the next User Story.

Acceptance Criteria and Scenarios

Whether your organization subscribes to ATDD/BDD or not, Acceptance Testing is critical in Lean and Agile development.

To facilitate Acceptance Tests, each User Story must have Acceptance Criteria (a.k.a. Conditions of Satisfaction) and Acceptance Tests defined before developers start coding.

These Acceptance Tests define conditions, functionality, data, and business rules the User Story must satisfy to be accepted by the Stakeholders. End conditions in Acceptance Tests determine when a User Story is consider complete and working correctly.

Although there are several different approaches for writing and structuring Acceptance Tests (e.g. unstructured User Story Acceptance Criteria, Scenarios, Test Cases, etc.), in most organizations we encountered Scenarios written in Gherkin's GIVEN-WHEN-THEN (GWT) language. Many Agile teams use GWT Scenarios because the transition to automated testing becomes much easier.

Scenario: **Fred requests recommended training topics**

GIVEN **Fred is logged in to website**
     And **Fred has completed BASE**
     And **Fred has unfinished training topics**
WHEN **Fred requests training plan**
THEN   **Fred's customized training plan is viewable**

Lean/Agile approaches recognize that GWT Scenarios developed for Acceptance Testing **ARE** the real requirements from the developers' perspective. Because of that, we develop Scenarios **BEFORE** writing the code. This is critical for the success of Agile/Lean undertakings.

Where do you start Scenario identification?

Finding the right Scenarios for Acceptance Testing is one of the more challenging tasks. There are several different techniques for finding Scenarios depending on which source you use (i.e. User Stories, Features, Decision Tables, Problem Statements, Use Cases, and other artifacts).

Here are the most commonly used techniques:

From User Stories to Scenarios

The most common method to creating Scenarios is to use brainstorming techniques finding Scenarios based on the business value (the WHY) and the business need (the WHAT) of the User Story.

Brainstorm for 5 minutes and list all different situations that you can think of that would confirm that the product does what it should do.

If your User Story has qualifiers such as: "As a visitor, I can view **all available** flights that fit my scheduling constraints to select the best fit", brainstorm Scenarios targeting the qualifier.

From Business Rules to Scenarios

Business Rules can easily lead you to several Scenarios. However, it is exceedingly difficult to extrapolate the different possible outcomes of a complex Business Rule.

Decision Tables allow you to express complex Business Rules. Once you have created a Decision Table, it is easy to identify critical Scenarios or Scenario Outlines. They are right there in front of you. Each column in a Decision Table is at least ONE Scenario!

From Pain-Point Analysis Outcomes to Scenarios

If you did a Pain-Point Analysis as described in an earlier chapter, you can use the outcomes of this analysis to create Scenarios quickly. The primary test of any implemented User Story or Feature is that, if the Feature or Story works correctly, the problems (Pain-Points) and associated symptoms go away!

To prove that a specific symptom has disappeared, you can write a GIVEN-WHEN-THEN Scenario or Scenario Outline targeting that symptom.

From Use Cases to Scenarios

A Use Case is another phenomenal tool for getting to Scenarios. It is a simple transition. When you analyze a Use Case for Test Scenario development, you can create a positive Scenario for each Standard, Alternate, and Exception Path to prove that they work.

The purpose of a positive Scenario is to prove that Standard and Alternate Paths deliver the same Post-conditions and that each Exception Path delivers its Post-conditions.

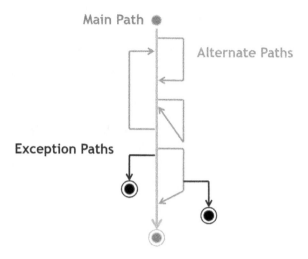

You can also create negative Scenarios. A negative Scenario ensures that your Feature or User Story gracefully handles wrong Pre-conditions, invalid data input or unexpected user behavior. Use your creativity to imagine what an end-user could do wrong.

From Functional Features to Scenarios

You can even find Scenarios using Functional Features discovered during Story Decomp / Feature Drill-down, a technique that we mentioned in an earlier chapter. This is a powerful method for finding Scenarios once the team is working at a low level of detail, meaning just before coding.

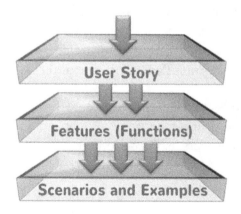

From Non-Functional Requirements to Scenarios

Non-functional testing is as important as functional testing. If you want to ensure customer satisfaction do not neglect writing Scenarios that test NFRs of the product as well.

There are Global NFRs that will span the whole product such as architectural requirements. You or someone else needs to write Scenarios for them. However, if a new Story needs a specific NFR, you will most likely be tasked to define one or more Scenarios for it.

Global NFRs are often implemented early in an initiative. Therefore, check to see that the NFRs extracted from a User Story are not covered by an existing Test Scenarios before you define any new ones. Perhaps there is an existing automated or manual Acceptance Test to verify these NFRs.

You can create tests for NFRs in the form of Acceptance Criteria, Scenarios, or just as artifacts. NFRs always should be split from a User Story since they often need to be tested at various times throughout the product lifecycle.

Test Data Engineering

Test Data Engineering is about identifying the best data values for each Acceptance Test or Scenario. If you randomly pick data input values, you will end up with a thundering herd of Scenarios. You have no idea whether you covered the most critical outcomes.

Test Data Engineering makes the testing process Lean and repeatable which results in effective regression testing. It will:

- ☑ minimize the number of Acceptance Tests
- ☑ make the process of testing repeatable
- ☑ support Regression Testing

Beyond saving time by developing as few Scenarios as possible, Regression Testing is yet another reason we need to engineer test data. How does Regression Testing work?

GWT Scenarios will be executed repeatedly. Every time a developer makes a change to the application, all previously accepted Scenarios used to test the current product or application will be run again.

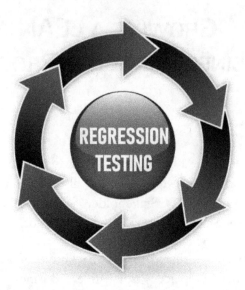

This process is called Regression Testing. That is a critical and often overlooked goal of Acceptance Testing.

When you are testing the latest release, having regression tests will save you a lot of time and headache. Regression testing allows you to re-test everything that you had already tested in earlier releases making sure that the newly developed features did not break anything. This is the core of implementing ATDD/BDD.

Author's Note: For some of you, this brief overview of business analysis techniques will be enough to get you started. If you want more guidance how to apply the described techniques, check out our book "Getting and Writing IT Requirements in a Lean and Agile World - Business Analysis Techniques for Discovering User Stories, Features, and Gherkin (Given-When-Then) Scenarios". You can find it on our website or on amazon (https://amzn.to/2jMQKTL).

GROWING A LEAN
BUSINESS ANALYSIS PROCESS

Summary

We have given you a definition of Lean and Agile principles, philosophies, and methodologies. We also explained the shift in deliverables from Business, Stakeholder, Solution-level Requirements to Features, User Stories, Examples, and Scenarios.

The various Backlogs that form the backbone of Lean analysis are repositories that replace exhaustive Business Requirements Documents.

The sections on Lean and Agile Analysis techniques introduced many new ways of getting, communicating, and managing the new requirements constructs. We tried to keep our descriptions simple and therefore lacking specific details to keep this an overview of the topic. If we whetted your appetite on any of the techniques, we encourage you to google it for more details.

Once you start to create and use Vision Statements, Minimal Viable Products, Cynefin, Stacey Matrices, Pain-Point Analysis, etc., you will discover even more ways of staying true to the Lean principles. In our opinion, the move toward ATDD and BDD may be the most significant improvement in Business Analysis since the inception of this evolving field.

That is fundamentally our take on how to make Business Analysis activities Lean and Agile. We do not pretend to have written the last word on the topic, but we hope this book has jump-started your thinking about how to eliminate waste from your Business Analysis practices.

A word of caution: too often Lean thinking focuses on the elimination of waste at the expense of quality of product. It is important to emphasize that

---

lean processes maximize the value to the customer while minimizing waste by building quality in from the start.

Quality of product cannot be integrated after the fact, so while you are improving your BA activities, do not throw the baby out with the bathwater.

In our experience, your primary focus should be on delivering requirements with the essential quality first and eliminating waste second. Only if the outcome has that level of quality can you really achieve a lean process over time.:

Where do you go from here?

First off, if you are a skilled business analyst, apply your skills to your own Business Analysis process:

- ☑ Create a **product** called "Business Analysis".

- ☑ Use Pain-Point / problem analysis techniques to identify deficiencies in your process.

- ☑ Work with stakeholders to ensure that you have multiple perspectives on the issues that cause you to waste resources.

- ☑ Use your analysis skills to define the requirements for an efficient and effective Lean Business Analysis process.

As the one wearing the BA hat, your product (your BA process) consists of requirements in any form that define the future business solution including software. Every step of your Business Analysis process must add value to that product.

Strive for Lean requirements in your requirements discovery work. Make sure that your requirements are at the level of detail needed for imminent decisions.

The ultimate quality test for a requirement is whether it allows a common interpretation by all relevant stakeholders. That is true whether you are writing User Stories, Feature Lists, Test Scenarios, or simple sentence requirements.

Do not spend a lot of time documenting the requirements to a level of detail that nobody is ever going to read.

Get a Lean, Mean Business Needs Communication Machine

Lean and Agile forms express business needs as User Stories, Epics, Features, Lean Use Cases, and Lean Requirements. These are modern techniques for capturing and communicating requirements. They are the basis for a lean, mean business needs communication machine.

By applying the principles of Lean to your Business Analysis process, you will be able to deliver higher quality. You are going to find that your work becomes a lot more effective and more efficient. You can get more done in less time.

Just as a reminder, here are the six basic Lean principles that you can use for any process or workflow to make them more efficient while adding value.

1. Deliver Appropriate Details Just-in-Time (JIT)
2. Deliver Only What Is Needed and Not More
3. Work with the Right People at the Right Time
4. Build Quality in From the Outset
5. Avoid Unnecessary Non-Value Adding Activities
6. Practice Active Collaboration and Knowledge Sharing

You might want to print this list out as a memory tickler and post if visibly in your workspace. In our experience, keeping this list visible helps serve as a trigger for action.

AUTHORS' NOTE:

This book serves to introduce the concept of Lean Business Analysis. If you would like to learn the details of how to capture, analyze, and communicate Lean requirements, get our book, "Getting and Writing IT Requirements in a Lean and Agile World" (https://amzn.to/2jMQKTL).